THE BEAUTY APOTHECARY

THE BEAUTY

APOTHECARY

Soulful Remedies to Foster Beauty Inside and Out

L'ORRIANE ANDERSON

ROCKPOOL

A Rockpool book
PO Box 252
Summer Hill
NSW 2130
Australia

rockpoolpublishing.com
Follow us! rockpoolpublishing
Tag your images with #rockpoolpublishing

ISBN: 9781923208018

Published in 2026 by Rockpool Publishing

Design and typesetting by Sara Lindberg, Rockpool Publishing
Edited by Lisa Macken
Images from Shutterstock

A catalogue record for this book is available from the National Library of Australia

A note about the recipes

This book uses US cup and spoon measures.
1 teaspoon = 5 ml
1 tablespoon = 15 ml
1 cup = approximately 240 ml

Printed and bound in China
10 9 8 7 6 5 4 3 2 1

CONTENTS

INTRODUCTION

What does *living beautifully* mean?

When I set out to write this book, my mind drifted to just one thing: looking beautiful. Originally it was divided into two parts, inner and outer beauty with the intention being a book to help you look and feel your best. I went to the manuscript again and again, trying to force out recipes to serve this purpose, and each time I felt my soul pushing back at me. Imagine you just arrived in a hotel room and started to unpack your things, only to have someone pick your stuff up and throw them back into your suitcase. Like someone said, what you have doesn't belong here. That's how writing the original version of this book felt: as though it was in the wrong place and time.

After a conversation with a dear friend – thank you, Tenae, for listening to me complain and helping me work through my thoughts – I realized writing a book about looking beautiful did feel out of place. There's absolutely nothing wrong with wanting to look your best, but I have come to realize the ways in which we approach beauty are changing. Beauty isn't just about how you look or even how you feel; beauty is about embodying what uplifts, inspires, grounds, and nurtures you and brings you a sense of harmony.

It's that sensation you have when looking at a painting or piece of art that speaks directly to your soul, or when you hear a song that brings you to joyful tears every time you hear it. Beauty is in the moments when the sunset is an unusually gorgeous shade of orange and purple, or when you take that first sip of tea and your whole body feels like it's defrosting, warming from the inside out. Beauty is about having a clear mind as much as it is about having clear skin or a radiant home, and as much as it is about you having a youthful glow. It's a way of being your full self, every single day, in whatever way feels most beautiful to you.

Living beautifully simply means living intentionally and authentically. This book has evolved from a very simplistic view of beauty to a much more elevated and elegant version. Without me knowing it, this book taught me how to live beautifully. I had to be authentic to myself before I could write a beautiful book. I had to acknowledge that for me, beauty extends far beyond good hair and makeup or self-care baths. Once I listened to this truth I found beauty poured onto these pages with ease, and the result is what you hold in your hands: inspiration to live with purpose, fostering a life that feels just as good as it looks.

YOUR PERSONAL BEAUTY APOTHECARY

An apothecary is technically defined as a person or place that sells drugs or medicines. Over the years, apothecary has grown to mean a collection of remedies that provide healing and transformation. These days it's not uncommon to find an apothecary that promotes meditation and journaling in combination with elixirs and potions, or fragrant sprays and candles for the home right next to tonics and teas. When I use the word "apothecary" I mean a collection of soulful remedies that foster intention, harmony, and grace. That includes philosophies, rituals, tools, and inspiration just as much as teas, balms, baths, and other herbal preparations. It's a metaphorical apothecary if you will, meant to address both a tangible sense of beauty through your physical body and environment, as well as an intangible sense of beauty through your emotions and spiritual connection.

HOW TO USE THIS BOOK BEAUTIFULLY

This book is divided into three parts. The first, "The foundation of beauty," is where we'll explore beauty archetypes, or profiles you can use to discover your unique sense of beauty expression. I'll walk you through some ingredients you might wish to have on hand for creating your own in-home beauty apothecary and some general tips for using them.

The second part of the book is focused entirely on inner beauty. Here we will explore a beautiful mind, heart and soul and what I call the "beauty principles." There are three principles for each of the chapters, exploring a different aspect of what it means to be beautiful from the inside out. You will also find a selection of beauty allies, or what you might know as correspondences.

Essentially, these are ingredients that embody each of the beauty principles I've outlined. Use these ingredients when formulating your own beauty remedies, or as decoration to bring the essence of each principle to life in your space. You'll also find a wonderful selection of beauty remedies, aka recipes to make. Make them as is or use them as a base to create your beauty potions.

Finally, the third section is related to all things outer beauty: recipes to help you look your best. Here you'll discover recipes for hair and body, along with fragrances for both yourself and your space. I've purposefully made these recipes intention-less. This has nothing to do with energy; rather, these recipes are in the pursuit of pure and simple self-care and beauty. Additionally, you'll find my current selection of base recipes, which you can customize to fit your specific needs and intentions beauty related or otherwise. Some of these recipes may feel familiar if you're a fan of my previous work, but be sure to review them anyway as I often make small but meaningful improvements as time goes on.

PART I

THE FOUNDATION OF BEAUTY

Beauty is truly in the eye of the beholder, so what's beautiful to me may mean something entirely different to you. Therefore, it can be helpful to have an idea of your unique sense of beauty. In Part I you'll find 10 beauty archetypes, or what you might prefer to call beauty personality types, that are a fun way to see what beauty means to you. You'll likely have a general sense already but I find it helpful to have a profile or concept that feels more tangible, as this will give you a goal of sorts that you can use as a guiding light. Just remember that these archetypes are guidelines: they are not set in stone and you can expect your archetype to change with time, so be sure to revisit this chapter often.

This wouldn't be an apothecary book without some guidance on how to create your own apothecary, so you'll also find some inspiration for plants, oils, and other ingredients you might want to keep on hand.

CHAPTER 1

BEAUTY ARCHETYPES

Archetypes are a very standard representation of a specific person or thing, and are used to help us understand a concept or how a person might express themselves. We can also use archetypes as a sort of guiding light or metaphorical mentor, giving us a set of parameters in which to pattern ourselves. An archetype can apply to just about any realm of your life, but here they're adapted for the purposes of discovering what beauty means to you, what drains you of a sense of beauty, and how you can achieve more beauty in your life internally and externally.

You might have a natural ability to find beauty in new or unusual things such as the seeker archetype, or perhaps you're more like a protector and your unique sense of beauty is found in your strength. You will have a primary archetype; however, it's quite common to resonate with several archetypes, combining them to form your unique personality. Take the following quiz to see which archetype you resonate with most then turn to your primary archetype's profile on the following pages for inspiration on how to bring your natural sense of beauty to life. You can also take the interactive version of this quiz at spiritelement.co/beautyapothecary.

WHAT'S YOUR BEAUTY ARCHETYPE?

Circle one answer for each of the following questions, then at the end count how many times each archetype appeared in your answers. The archetype that appears the most is your primary archetype, but be sure to also read about the runner-up for a fuller picture of your unique beauty style.

1. WHAT DOES SELF-CARE MEAN TO YOU?

A. Tending to wounds, physical or emotional; your own or other people's.

B. Trying new techniques and evolving your routine, always seeking something better.

C. Seeking inspiration from the world, blending new trends and experiences.

D. Creating and showcasing beauty as art; you love to stand out.

E. Keeping things simple, stable, and reliable; you thrive on order and peace.

F. Rituals that connect you with spirit or deepen your intuition.

G. Luxurious rituals that make you feel powerful, worthy, and regal.

H. Connecting with loved ones; feeling beautiful is being loved and loving others.

I. Doing what feels good in the moment, embracing freedom and rawness.

J. Prioritizing physical vitality such as exercise and nourishment, and glowing radiance.

2. YOUR HOME MOST LOOKS LIKE:

A. DIYs, restored objects, and plants; everything has a story.

B. Ever-evolving vignettes and experimental arrangements.

C. Eclectic treasures and souvenirs from your travels.

D. Art, color, and bold designs; you love to be surrounded by beautiful things.

E. Calm, tidy spaces with timeless staples and practical storage.

F. Altars, crystals, and spiritual décor; your sanctuary.

G. Luxe fabrics, a signature scent, and curated design objects.

H. Warm, inviting spaces filled with sentimental treasures and photos.

I. Mismatched finds, unconventional furniture, and a bit of beautiful chaos.

J. Open, airy rooms with minimal pieces and plenty of natural light.

3. WHAT BEST DESCRIBES YOUR APPROACH TO STYLE AND BEAUTY?

A. Natural, holistic, and nurturing; DIY is your love language.

B. Always trying new things and refining your look.

C. Adventurous, following your curiosity and intuition.

D. Creative, expressive, and sometimes a bit over the top.

E. Functional, reliable, and fuss free.

F. Intentional, spiritual, and energetically aligned.

G. Refined, confidence building, and meticulously put together.

H. Soft, inviting, and focused on enhancing natural beauty.

I. Free-spirited, unconventional, and ever-changing.

J. Clean and radiant, and focused on health and vitality.

4. IN A GROUP YOU'RE THE ONE WHO:

A. Listens deeply and offers support.

B. Brings new ideas or mixes things up.

C. Connects people from different groups.

D. Inspires and uplifts with your creativity.

E. Provides stability and practical advice.

F. Shares wisdom or spiritual insights.

G. Commands attention and leads with confidence.

H. Makes everyone feel included and cherished.

I. Breaks the mold or surprises everyone.

J. Encourages movement or brings fresh energy.

5. WHAT DRAINS YOUR ENERGY OR DIMS YOUR SENSE OF BEAUTY?

A. Over-giving, losing yourself in other people's needs.

B. Perfectionism and not knowing when to stop.

C. Feeling stuck or uninspired.

D. A lack of validation or creative blocks.

E. Too much change or pressure to be different.

F. Disconnection from spirit, feeling ungrounded.

G. Feeling unseen or not respected.

H. Disconnection or feeling unloved.

I. Rigidity or routine, loss of freedom.

J. Poor health or lack of physical energy.

6. YOUR IDEAL BEAUTY RITUAL IS:

A. Herbal teas, restorative baths, or tending to plants.

B. Mixing potions, experimenting with ingredients.

C. Trying a beauty trend.

D. Painting, dressing up, or creating a signature look.

E. Five-minute face routine, favorite lotion, done.

F. Meditation, smudging, and anointing oils.

G. Silk robes, luxury serums, and signature scent.

H. Face masks and hair treatments, and a friend or partner to share it with.

I. A spontaneous dance party or wildflower crown.

J. Morning movement, superfood smoothies and facial massages.

7. YOU FEEL MOST BEAUTIFUL WHEN:

A. You're fully present, your needs are met and you can help others.

B. You've mastered something unique or refined your look in a new way.

C. You're exploring someplace new or discovering something unexpected.

D. All eyes are on you: you've curated a look and moment worth remembering.

E. Everything is in its place and you feel calm, grounded, and put together.

F. You're aligned with your spirit, flowing with energy and in tune with your intuition.

G. You've taken time to honor yourself: you feel elegant, empowered, and in control.

H. You're surrounded by people you love, feeling adored and connected.

I. You've let go of expectations and followed your instincts.

J. Your body feels radiant, clear, and energized, like you're glowing from within.

ANSWERS

Mostly As: healer

Mostly Bs: alchemist

Mostly Cs: seeker

Mostly Ds: muse

Mostly Es: protector

Mostly Fs: mystic

Mostly Gs: sovereign

Mostly Hs: lover

Mostly Is: wild one

Mostly Js: luminary

THE HEALER

The healer finds beauty through nurturing, compassion, and empathy.

Inner beauty

The healer archetype finds beauty through the acceptance and nourishment of themselves, others, and the world around them. They are very good listeners, listening with their whole body and not just their ears. They sense and feel rather than attempting to justify with words. Their superpower is that they don't judge, making them easy to love and be around. They will approach every situation with a desire to understand, and that ability to hold space for forgiveness and compassion allows them to radiate a natural, almost ethereal warmth.

How the healer fosters beauty

- They are deeply aware and empathetic to their needs and those of the people around them.
- They are masters of restorative living: they're always seeking ways to foster peace and restore harmony and balance.
- They find beauty in all things, especially people and things that are easily dismissed or disregarded by others.

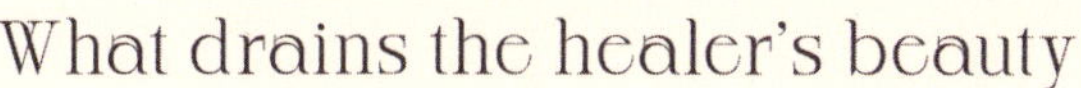

What drains the healer's beauty

- Although aware of their own needs, they tend to dismiss their personal needs in favor of helping others heal.
- Their deep sense of empathy sometimes means they can't separate their feelings from those of others. They often hold on to responsibilities and experiences that are not their own.
- Because they find beauty in all things, they can often take on more than they can realistically handle. They may fall victim to a martyr mentality, trying to save things that are well and truly beyond repair.

Outer beauty

The healer archetype is very in tune with the natural world. They prefer sustainable and natural materials whenever possible. They tend to avoid anything that's too precious, believing that beauty is something that should be lived in and enjoyed and that beauty should evolve, expressing its unique characteristics in all stages of its life. Someone with a healer archetype may include fresh flowers, then dry them and use them in a new way. Their natural eagerness to heal extends beyond the body. You find them restoring old furniture, thrifting and mending worn clothes, or filling their space with beloved heirlooms.

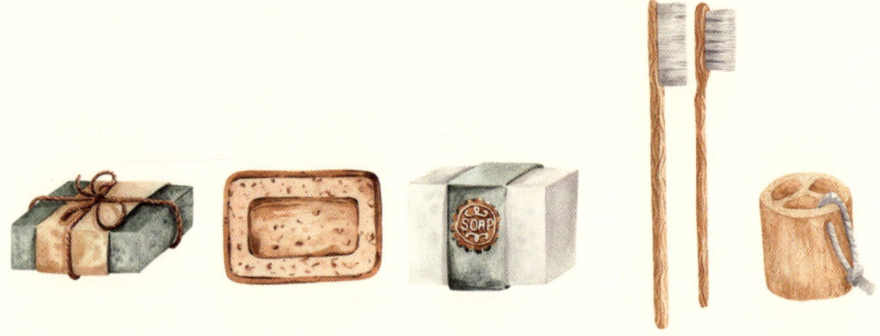

Best beauty strategies if you're a healer

- Make your own beauty care whenever possible, spending time connecting deeply with the ingredients used in your preparations.
- Practice setting boundaries. Make it a point to say "No" to someone at least once a day, especially anyone who expects more out of you than they give in return.

- Consider offering your healing skills to other things besides people. Work with animals, repair abandoned furniture, or renovate an old house.

Beauty restoration for the healer

- Make self-care a dedicated practice by scheduling it, giving yourself enough time to revive your spirit after so much time caring for everyone else.
- Nourish your body with healing ingredients and nourishing teas, and by drinking plenty of infused water.
- Ask for help when you're feeling drained or overwhelmed. The people around you may not realize how much you need support, especially when you are always rushing to be there for others.

Beautiful remedies for the healer

- Spirit ointment to uplight energy (page 91).
- Spiritual well-being bath vinegar (page 119).
- Spirit of beauty body lotion (page 181).
- Self-worship perfume (page 196).

THE ALCHEMIST

The alchemist finds beauty in evolution. They love the process of growing, expanding, and reinvention.

Inner beauty

The alchemist archetype loves to experiment, and nothing thrills them more than stumbling on something then refining the process. They are ever in the pursuit of mastery, always curious and eager to learn more. If they decide they love minimal styles, they will do everything in their power to embody this expression. To them, beauty is the pursuit of perfection and there is always something they can improve. Although they love to learn, they can sometimes get stuck in rules they've created for themselves, often limiting their growth.

How the alchemist fosters beauty

- They believe beauty is something that can evolve over time. Their desire to seek the purest expression of beauty makes them magnetic and mysterious, attracting others to their unique sense of style.
- Alchemists are unexpected: just when you think you've understood their expression of beauty, it evolves and the rules change.
- They always seem to have their pulse on some independent or quiet artisan, brand, or idea. They regularly seek out things that are different from others, blending styles to form something new.

What drains the alchemist's beauty

- Seeking perfection means the work is never done. The alchemist archetype may find it hard to find the finish line, burning themselves out or stressing over insignificant details.
- They can get lost in the process of beauty rather than the enjoyment of it. They may feel as though beauty is something they must do instead of something they enjoy doing.
- They love to be different and will often evolve just for the sake of standing as a unique individual. Nothing upsets them more than someone wearing the same thing or doing things in the same way. Because of this they may have trouble accepting what they love, feeling as though they have to evolve when too many others follow their lead.

Outer beauty

The alchemist has a dedicated and singular sense of style. They are the types to blend styles such as "maximal minimalist," creating a lane that is uniquely their own to master. However, you will notice a distinct pattern in how they approach beauty. Once they find something they love they will seek to repeat and perfect it. Thus, they may have a uniform or specific outfit formula they regularly wear, a dedicated makeup routine that rarely changes for long periods of time, or a specific self-care routine.

Best beauty strategies if you're an alchemist

- Take things one step at a time: there's no need to refine everything all at once. Likewise, experiment with one thing at a time, giving yourself enough space to fully understand the results of your experimentation.
- Experiment with your beauty routine. Layer unexpected beauty products or use them in new ways. Add unusual pops of color or textures to your wardrobe, or try making something no one else has.
- Align your beauty with something cyclical such as the seasons, moon phases, or zodiac signs. Doing so will give you a sense of mastering a system that you can then repeat again and again.

Beauty restoration for the alchemist

- Check in with your routine from time to time to evaluate what's working and what isn't, especially during seasonal changes.
- Learn to accept things as they are, including yourself. As an alchemist you may put too much pressure on yourself to be unique.
- Share your unique sense of style with others. Becoming a teacher or guide will force you to master your craft while also giving you space to experiment and grow.

Beautiful remedies for the alchemist

- Self-devotion perfume (page 132).
- Relaxing bathing cordial (page 184).
- Floral creme and spice botanical perfume (page 200).
- Self-serenity diffuser blend (page 210).

THE SEEKER

The seeker finds beauty by maintaining an open mind and allowing themselves to be inspired.

Inner beauty

The seeker archetype loves to be inspired and the feeling of discovery, often finding beauty in the unusual or things that are rare and precious. They have a natural curiosity that frequently takes them to new places or experiences. Their superpower is the ability to draw connections between seemingly different things. They have an uncanny ability to bring together different kinds of people, patterns, or ideas in a uniformed and harmonious way. Others look to them for guidance, knowing they will try all of the new stuff and weed out the bad.

How the seeker fosters beauty

- They bring a fresh perspective to old or competing ideas.
- They have an eagerness to learn, and their curiosity is often infectious.
- They welcome change, allowing themselves to stay open to any possibility for growth and transformation.

What drains the seeker's beauty

- They can lack grounding and stability. A consistent desire for change or new experiences can lead to burnout and overwhelm, or they may appear flighty and irresponsible.
- Their constant need to evolve can sometimes alienate them from other people, who may find it challenging to know what to expect from this archetype and leave them feeling unlovable or misunderstood.
- They tend to be a jack of all trades, missing out on opportunities to master something meaningful or beneficial to them.

Outer beauty

The seeker archetype loves a new trend, especially something in its nascent stages. They're adventurous with their style, having no problem experimenting with new and unusual ways to express themselves – and how they express themselves evolves often. They may love minimalism and neutral colors today then switch to maximalism and bright, rich tones tomorrow. Because they are so easily inspired, they can find something beautiful in just about any combination of color, texture, composition, or style.

Best beauty strategies if you're a seeker

- Try out new beauty and style trends often. You're likely to find the next big thing long before most people, which means you always look your best.
- Don't be afraid to stand apart from the crowd. You may feel alienated at times, but try to view it as leadership more so than loneliness. There are plenty of people who look to you for guidance and inspiration.

Beauty restoration for the seeker

- Practice grounding yourself rather than always flying to the next thing. This will give your body time to catch up to your restless spirit, and allow you to recharge your energy. Consider creating a grounding ritual you can come back to again and again to stay balanced among the constant change. Alternatively, you can make grounding a routine. You might do something to ground yourself every Saturday but how you go about it still changes, such as a nature walk one week and a yoga practice the next.
- Deeply invest and master something such as how you style your hair, wardrobe, perhaps a room of your house or the types of foods you eat, such as dedicating yourself to being a vegan. This will help to combat restlessness and balance your energy rather than spreading it too thin.

Beautiful remedies for the seeker

- Retreat: herbal bathing salts for contemplation and soul work (page 85).
- Angel's light body and anointing oil (page 130).
- Self-expression diffuser blend (page 211).

THE MUSE

The muse loves beauty for beauty's sake. They adore more traditional expressions of beauty such as art, and they thrive with external validation.

Inner beauty

The muse archetype is quite playful in their expression of beauty. They love to be seen and will often try bold, dramatic looks and practices to be the center of attention. Like the seeker and the alchemist, they are no strangers to experimentation. They are naturally creative and ingenious, often coming up with unique combinations and methods. However, they can feel depleted when their beauty isn't validated, or when they aren't in the midst of creative expression.

How the muse fosters beauty

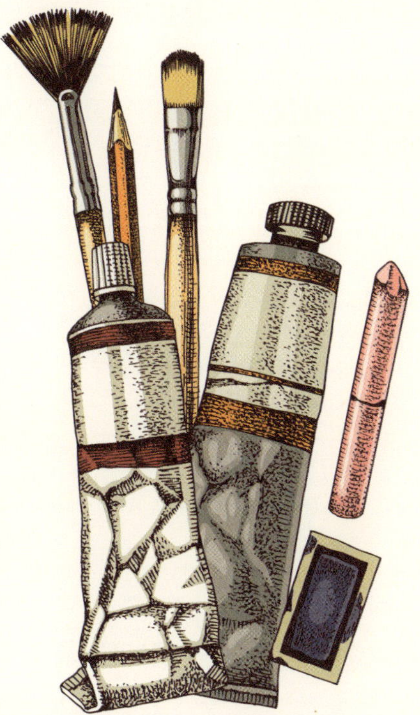

- Their natural creative nature allows them to find beauty in fresh ideas.
- They tend to be extroverts and love to inspire others.
- They see their entire being as art, making them confident and expressive. They are a masterpiece, and they encourage others to see themselves the same way.

What drains the muse's beauty

- They can feel undervalued or insecure when others do not validate their beauty choices.
- Creativity is often tied to their mood: any gaps in creative expression can leave them feeling unmotivated and moody.
- Putting too much emphasis on being beautiful or expressing beauty can mean other things in their life are neglected.

Outer beauty

The muse archetype loves beauty in all forms. You will find their home filled with art, from paintings to sculpture to bold furniture pieces. The same is true when it comes to what they wear: they will often try avant-garde clothing or choose a style that can feel a little over the top, such as wearing a ball gown to cocktail parties. They love the feeling of being bold and being recognized for it. When it comes to self-care, they want any and everything that will contribute to a sense of being beautiful even if it means trying non-conventional methods.

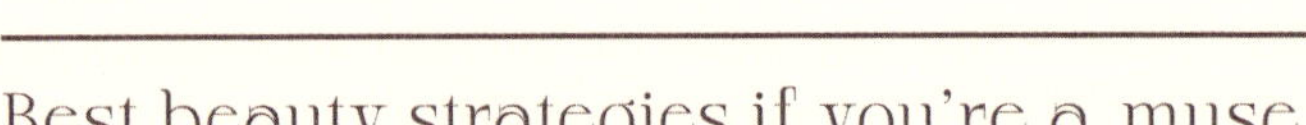

Best beauty strategies if you're a muse

- Consider sharing your beauty expertise with the world, as you'll be the center of attention and have an open space to try bold creative looks.
- Draw inspiration from other forms of art. Channel sculpture in your clothing choices or try a hairstyle from a 17th-century painting. Doing so will fuel your creativity and help you stand out from the crowd.
- Study art and beauty from different cultures and time periods. Beauty is a wide subject, and there's always a new way to be inspired.

Beauty restoration for the muse

- Focus more on inner validation rather than seeking attention. You will radiate even more brightly when you feel secure within yourself.
- Try to seek balance. Being bold is great, but it can be overwhelming at times. Consider featuring one bold thing: graphic eyeliner, a pop of color with a bright shirt, or having glass skin and minimal makeup.
- Ground your energy in the everyday. Schedule time to tackle mundane tasks that have nothing to do with beauty to make sure everything gets done.

Beautiful rituals for the muse

- Venusian beauty water (page 103).
- Apple harvest hair conditioner (page 170).
- Playful jasmine tincture perfume (page 192).

THE PROTECTOR

The protector finds beauty in stability and cultivating safe spaces. They seek peace and reliability and have a strong sense of who they are and what they like, which they will protect at all costs.

Inner beauty

The protector archetype thrives on stable and practical forms of beauty. They don't fix things that aren't broken, preferring to stay with what works for them. They have a strong sense of self: they know what they like and don't compromise on who they are, so it's very easy for them to have boundaries. For them, beauty means the bills are paid and dishes are done, and they can sleep soundly at night knowing there are no fires to put out.

How the protector fosters beauty

- They know who they are, what their style is, and their needs and wants. Their sense of self is grounded and cemented.
- They are warriors of peace: they don't overcomplicate things, always approaching situations with practicality.
- Their model is function over form. Things need to work, plain and simple.

What drains the protector's beauty

- They may lack self-care, finding it shallow and frivolous. They may not have a way to replenish themselves after challenging times or when facing burnout.
- They can become stagnant without any desire to experiment.
- Although they have a strong sense of self, protectors can miss out on the spirit of beauty. Everything doesn't need to have a function to have value or contribute to a feeling of peace.

Outer beauty

The protector likes to keep things simple, preferring things that are low maintenance and dependable. This is the type that is most likely to wear very little or no makeup, their beauty-care routine will have the least number of steps possible, and they may be prone to wearing neutrals or have a uniform or capsule-style wardrobe. However, they will invest in quality pieces and products that work well and can stand the test of time. They also tend to like things that are multi-function, such as a moisturizer that also has sunscreen or using a bar of soap that can work for face, body and hair. Protectors are all less likely to try DIY beauty products.

Best beauty strategies if you're a protector

- Keep things minimal. Invest in quality staple products from brands you know and trust.
- Focus on healing and nourishing products that set a strong foundation and promote long-term wellness.

Beauty restoration for the protector

- Allow yourself to be vulnerable and connect with the emotional or spiritual aspects of beauty. Find yourself in a song, or get lost studying the brush strokes of a painting that calls to you. Focusing on form over function will give you a break from needing everything to serve a purpose, and open your mind to new forms of well-being.
- See beauty as the ultimate expression of self-energy. You have a strong sense of self, but there is always room for growth. Consider reflecting on your favorite colors, patterns, textures, or beauty concepts to see if there is deeper insight to be had.
- Set yourself parameters to determine when you'll re-evaluate your beauty routine. Make it a part of your regular responsibilities so you have a regular check-in, adjusting as needed.

Beautiful remedies for the protector

- Indulgent self-love bath elixir (page 108).
- Invigorating body butter (page 182).
- Self-expression diffuser blend (page 211).

THE MYSTIC

The mystic finds beauty in inner wellness and spiritual connection. Beauty is deeply connected with their intuition, and brings a sense of love and gratitude to everything they do.

Inner beauty

The mystic archetype is deeply connected with their spiritual nature. For them beauty radiates from the inside out, and anything they do on the outside is a result of spiritual insight and reflection. They express their beauty from the heart, and beauty that serves practical and spiritual purposes. They enjoy things that have intention and energy, and connect them with the bigger picture.

How the mystic fosters beauty

- They check in with their spirit for every choice. They are very intentional, always seeking things that bring them closer to their soul essence.
- They spend time meditating, journaling, grounding, and the like. Inner wellness is their source of radiance.
- They always seem to be at peace or know the right thing to say. Their self-awareness helps them stay calm and balanced at all times.

What drains the mystic's beauty

- They can come across as superior or philosophical, often describing beauty as something unattainable or limited to very few.
- They can sometimes lack a connection with the world around them, focusing too much on spiritual pursuits and divine connection. They may need to ground their energy in the everyday, learning to appreciate outer beauty as much as inner beauty.
- They tend to value products with spiritual intentions more so than function. They will continue to purchase a crystal-infused face elixir just because it promotes a feeling of love, even if the product itself doesn't actually help their skin.

Outer beauty

The mystic loves mystical things. They enjoy the beauty of the cosmos, the earth, and other forms of spiritual or esoteric elements. They also tend to enjoy ethereal items that have a sense of whimsy or give them a priestess-like feeling. There is a regality about their style that makes them radiate deep inner wisdom. They enjoy things that are light, airy, and easy to move around in. They tend to engage in many spiritual endeavors, and don't enjoy feeling restricted.

Best beauty strategies if you're a mystic

- Make your beauty routine a ritual, even if products aren't infused with intention. Focus on the sacred act of caring for yourself as a spiritual experience.
- Align your beauty routine with the seasons, signs, moon phases, or sabbats.
- Find beauty products that are intentional but also working, ensuring you are glowing from the inside and out.

Beauty restoration for the mystic

- Find your own spiritual connections with product ingredients rather than needing someone to tell you what it's for. A product with rose water carries the vibration of love even if it isn't dedicated for that purpose, or a product with lavender could correspond with the feeling of peace. Drawing your own correspondences will allow you to channel your inner wisdom while also finding effective remedies.
- Take a break from spiritual pursuits, even if only for a day. You are a spiritual being, but you are here to have a human experience. It's important to give your intuition space from time to time.
- Focus on other forms of self-care such as nourishing your body, drinking more water, exercising, or connecting with people in your life.

Beautiful remedies for the mystic

- Grounded sleep linen powder (page 129).
- Sacred adornment dedication ritual (page 146).
- Soft as roses body wash (page 180).
- Smoked vanilla and pine perfume (page 190).

THE SOVEREIGN

The sovereign finds beauty in their confidence, authority, and ability to command respect from others.

Inner beauty

The sovereign archetype is the most confident of all the archetypes. Their beauty comes from within, from their deep love and respect for themselves. They view taking care of themselves as an expression of their sacredness and have a strong sense of self, almost to a fault, and will not compromise when it comes to their self-care. They are elegant, refined, and sometimes quite assertive as well. Because they are such a natural authority they can struggle with projecting their idea of beauty onto others.

How the sovereign fosters beauty

- They view themselves as sacred in everything they do.
- They respect themselves to a fault and expect the same level of respect from others, which of course means they usually get it.
- They view self-care as a need, not a luxury. Taking care of themselves is non-negotiable.

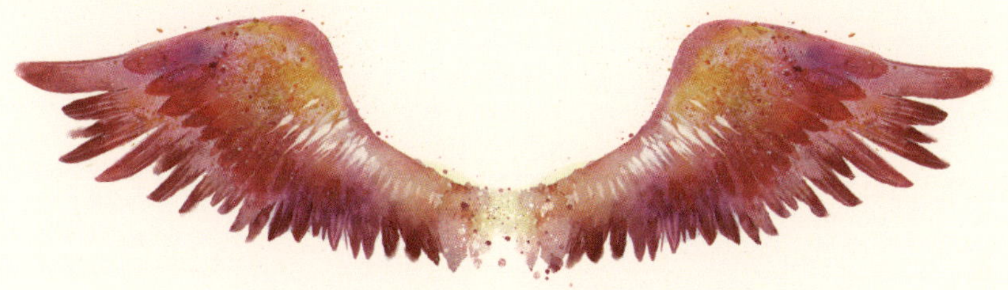

What drains the sovereign's beauty

- They can sometimes look down on other expressions of beauty that do not match their own. This can make them seem like a tyrant or bully, or make them appear less beautiful to others.
- Their deep self-love can come across as arrogant or self-absorbed.
- They can lack vulnerability. They associate beauty with power, which means they can sometimes lack softness and grace.

Outer beauty

The sovereign archetype drips luxury, loving to have the best of the best: the best fabrics and materials, ingredients, experiences, and so on. They invest in themselves in every way possible. They tend to have a very refined and curated style, having meticulously crafted themselves in their idea of beauty. You will know their sense of style when you see it. Everything from their home to wardrobe to makeup and hair, even the kind of people they have in their life, will feel curated and consistent. They also tend to have an incredible eye for detail.

Best beauty strategies if you're a sovereign

- Develop your signature style, such as a bold lipstick or distinctive fragrance you wear every day, or being known for wearing driving gloves.
- Embrace rituals for self-worth and empowerment. Seeing yourself as sacred on a regular basis will help to solidify your natural feeling that you are worthy of anything you desire.
- Seek out artisan, handcrafted pieces made with luxe materials. Investing in yourself in all ways will contribute to your sense of sacredness and value.

Beauty restoration for the sovereign

- Practice vulnerability and softness. Your power and strength will always be your calling card, but true beauty comes from accepting all parts of who you are.
- Give others space to express their sense of beauty, because doing so will allow you to find value in others and perhaps find new ways to express your own sense of self.
- Rest from time to time; you don't need to be done up every single day. Give yourself some dedicated time to have a more minimal routine. Embrace imperfections and let your hair down, literally.

Beautiful remedies for the sovereign

- Self-consecration body scrub (page 106).
- Ultra nourishing hair oil (page 164).
- Power perfume (page 194).

THE LOVER

The lover finds beauty in the people around them. Their relationships are very important to them, and they feel most beautiful when they are loved and supported.

Inner beauty

The lover archetype is a romantic, needing connection with others. Like the muse they need validation, and will go out of their way to be beautiful for the people they love. You can count on them to look their best at all times when engaged in a social setting, although they aren't shallow. To them, looking their best for you is a sign of their commitment to you. They also tend to be warm, charming, and openly emotional as well as deeply empathic.

How the lover fosters beauty

- They are engaged in those they care about. You will often get the sense you're the only person in the world when you're with them.
- They are only interested in meaningful relationships, and will invest the time and energy needed to build healthy, long-lasting connections.
- They exude kindness. They are the type that never meets a stranger, finding a way to connect with everyone they meet.

What drains the lover's beauty

- They can be people pleasers, and in doing so may lose themselves trying to fit someone else's ideas of beauty.
- They may lack boundaries as they love to feel deeply connected, which can make them come across as needy or lacking their own interests.
- They may struggle with insecurities if others do not validate their beauty or acknowledge their efforts.

Outer beauty

The lover archetype's aesthetic is very warm and inviting. They like things that are soft and ethereal, or even feminine. They tend to avoid bold choices, going with things that are safe or they know will be well received. They are always put together and refined, and tend to have a quite timeless style. They enjoy hair, makeup and clothes that are understated but pristine.

Best beauty strategies if you're a lover

- Embrace beauty remedies that align with the spirit of beauty. Incorporate products with ingredients such as rose, hibiscus, and violet to inspire a sense of warmth and softness.
- Enhance your natural radiance with beauty remedies for glowing hair and shiny skin. You already have a strong foundation, so now build upon it.

Beauty restoration for the lover

- Spend time alone in relationship with yourself. Your needs also matter, and you need time to take care of yourself and replenish your energy. Consider a solo candlelit dinner or a self-care day.
- Focus on self-love rituals, directing some of that romance toward yourself.
- Develop your own sense of style and identity rather than changing your style to suit others. Find something that is uniquely your own and incorporate it into your normal style.

Beautiful remedies for the lover

- Taking stock of your beautiful mind: an exercise in self-awareness (page 77).
- Self-centered: a ritual for a beautiful morning of falling back in love with yourself (page 101).
- Nectar body oil (page 187).

THE WILD ONE

The wild one finds beauty in freedom and the full expression of who they are. They are rooted in the present moment, and are governed by their feelings.

Inner beauty

The wild one archetype is raw, unfiltered, and unapologetically authentic. They go where their heart takes them, which is often very unconventional and unexpected. They completely renounce trends and the status quo. Their beauty is atypical, often viewed as being confusing or even disruptive, and they believe everyone should have the freedom to choose what they love. Their ability to accept their most raw nature means they are always accepting of others. They rarely judge and gravitate toward others with an unusual sense of style.

How the wild one fosters beauty

- They live in the moment. They can be very spontaneous, adventurous, and exciting, which draws people to them.
- They're authentic: what you see is what you get, and you can always count on them to be honest. They live for themselves and no one else, often quietly inspiring others to live more boldly.
- They're effortless. Everything they do seems easy and natural, mostly because they don't fuss. They simply do what feels good to them, giving them a light-hearted energy.

What drains the wild one's beauty

- They reject anything that is rigid or structured. They don't like routines, so they can lack a sense of grounding and commitment.
- Their spontaneous nature means they're often unprepared. They may not have the tools or products needed when necessary, forcing them to find alternatives in a pinch.
- Their rawness can sometimes come across as looking unkempt. They don't put as much value into things as others, so they may have a hard time taking care of themselves or their possessions.

Outer beauty

The wild one archetype has a truly unique style, often a mash of a lot of different styles in one: you can expect the unexpected from them. They tend to have eclectic approaches that are effortless and unpolished. Some wild ones may be clad in head-to-toe pink leather, while others may like to dress as 18th-century vampires. Their self-care routines may be just as wild, trying experimental products on a whim or foraging for ingredients to make in their own home.

Best beauty strategies if you're a wild one

- Make beauty remedies as you go, allowing you to customize based on your mood at the time. Have beauty bases at the ready to make the process easier and more efficient.
- Keep it simple. Because you are more spontaneous, layering too many beauty remedies can feel overwhelming. Choose one or two things to focus on at a time.
- Trust your instincts: if a beauty remedy feels right in the moment, then go with it.

Beauty restoration for a wild one

- Cultivate peace and serenity. Learn to be still in the moment and slow down, allowing your mind and body time to catch up with your spirit.
- Build deeper connections with others. Your spontaneous nature can make it challenging for others to connect with you on a deeper level, which means they don't get to see the full sense of your beautiful nature.
- Channel your raw instincts into other forms of beauty such as ceramics, cooking, and makeup, which will allow you to experiment when you feel inspired while also giving you a creative outlet.

Beautiful remedies for the wild one

- Peacefully grounded sleep ritual (page 122).
- Beauty bases (page 149).
- Honey vanilla perfume (page 197).
- Self-serenity diffuser blend (page 210).

THE LUMINARY

The luminary finds beauty in well-being and vitality. Taking care of their physical body is their desired path to looking and feeling their best.

Inner beauty

The luminary archetype values radiance and energy. They feel their best when they have a lot of vitality and can move their body with ease. This type is most likely to seek body perfection: they enjoy going to the gym and eating a clean diet, even if it means restricting themselves. They love to glow and focus on beauty remedies that give them a bright, youthful appearance. They are quite magnetic and love to inspire others to take care of themselves.

How the luminary fosters beauty

- Their source of beauty is food. They eat superfoods, drink lots of water, and focus on beauty from the inside out.
- They take care of their physical appearance: you'll always catch them doing some kind of exercise to get their body moving.
- They're charming and always seem to be on, ready to go at any moment.

What drains the luminary's beauty

- They can restrict themselves too much, choosing to avoid social engagements or indulging from time to time if it means it will break their diet or fitness routine.
- Their super strict lifestyle can feel overwhelming to some, causing them to miss out on meaningful connections.
- They don't prioritize spiritual beauty enough. They focus on inner beauty in the sense of what they eat, but may lack a feeling of connecting with a higher power or the bigger picture.

Outer beauty

The luminary archetype's style is anything that enhances their natural beauty. They love to glow and will wear things that feature their best characteristics, from face contour to workout leggings that show off their sculptured rear end. They are the ones who will do the 20-step beauty routine for glossy hair and radiant skin, as they have no problem with drawn-out routines.

Best beauty strategies if you're a luminary

- Create a morning ritual to set you up for the rest of the day. Drink water with electrolytes, do a quick workout routine, and take an uplifting bath or shower to start off the day fresh.
- Choose beauty remedies that uplift your spirit and match your natural energy.
- Invest in all products, from hair masks to serums to cuticle oils. You're most likely to put in the work, so go ahead and go all out.

Beauty restoration for the luminary

- Indulge from time to time by engaging the 80/20 rule: you're strict 80 percent of the time, but give yourself 20 percent of your time to enjoy the things you love.
- Prioritize spiritual connection, especially the darker or more challenging practices such as shadow work or self-compassion.

Beautiful remedies for the luminary

- Retreat: herbal bathing salts for contemplation and soul work (page 85).
- Spirit ointment to uplight energy (page 91).
- Restore your spirit daily ritual (page 121).
- The empress perfume (page 199).

CHAPTER 2

THE BEAUTY APOTHECARY

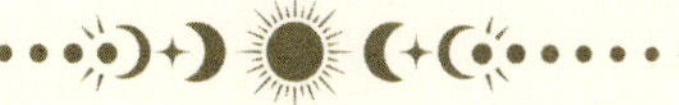

PLANTS AND HERBS

Plants and herbs are a key component in any apothecary, and not just for their intentions or healing benefits. Fortunately, there are now many online resources available to access even some of the rarest or most unusual plants and herbs. You can get plants in many different forms, from powders to dried herbs and even fresh herbs in some cases.

However, if you have a green thumb or wish to try gardening, then I would really recommend growing your own herbs and flowers. Not only is it better for the environment, but you can use these plants to bring a pop of beauty to your home. I have way too much parsley growing in my garden because it's one of my favorite herbs, but it also happens to make a beautiful bouquet when layered with other flowers. Once the herbs and flowers start to wilt they are dried and used for other things, bringing beauty into my space and practice in many different ways. When it comes to beauty, I recommend having at least the following herbs and flowers at hand:

- **Calendula:** a lovely bright flower that corresponds to the sun. It helps to unlock radiance in the spirit, promotes healing, and facilitates joy.
- **Hibiscus:** this expressive flower promotes love, beauty, and a sense of vitality. It encourages a zest for life and will help you express your unique essence.
- **Jasmine:** for boosting confidence and releasing the spiritual and emotional blocks that prevent you from fully expressing your spirit.
- **Lavender:** although commonly used for peace lavender also corresponds to love, helping to restore relationships of all kinds, including the relationship you have with yourself. It stimulates inspiration, especially in dreams, and encourages you to let go of negative thoughts and actions.
- **Peppermint:** mints in general, including spearmint and mugwort, are cleansing and protecting to the spirit. Peppermint helps remove blocks to self-worth and is often used to promote a sense of love.
- **Rose:** an overall emotional healer and comforting balm to the mind, body and soul. It facilitates peace, unlocks inspiration and inspires loyalty and love.
- **Violet:** often associated with peace, this dreamy flower also promotes self-expression and attracts love.

FRAGRANCE OILS

There was a time when I was totally against fragrance oils, but my opinion has changed over the years. For one, fragrance oils have really come a long way, meaning there are so many clean fragrance oils available. Also, the huge demand for herbs and essential oils has put a strain on availability and sustainability, so I am much more mindful these days to seek other options that aren't as taxing to the earth.

Aside from environmental concerns, I find that I really love the experience fragrance oils provide. They add a richness and depth to scent blends that isn't always achievable through essential oils alone, and when we're seeking the pursuit of beauty I think it's more important to have a beautiful fragrance than to worry about the energetic properties of your fragrance blend. Not to mention, there are many other ways to infuse your beauty potions with plant energy, leaving the fragrance free to be something pleasing to your nose. Any recipes that have essential oil blends – except for the diffuser blends – can be swapped with a fragrance blend of your choice. Just be sure to select fragrance oils that are safe for the skin, as some of them are not.

ESSENTIAL OILS

First and foremost, I do not advise taking essential oils internally *under any circumstances,* despite some online information suggesting otherwise. Essential oils are highly concentrated, and though they are plant based they are indeed chemical compounds. Taking the oils internally can lead to allergic reactions and interfere with medications, and may contribute to negative long-term effects.

When using them externally it's important to dilute them properly before applying to the skin, especially when used in a bath. Water disperses essential oils, and from my experience a few drops of undiluted essential oil – even one or two – can cause skin irritation and even burning. For the recipes in this book, generally 20 to 50 drops is enough for a 2 oz | 60 ml potion.

With that out of the way we can move on to the fun stuff, which is using essential oils to customize your beauty potions. Unlike fragrance oils, essential oils do have energetic properties such as self-love or self-worth. You can find a list of what essential oils to use in Part II of this book to help you decide which ones are right for your beauty remedy, but essential oils also have healing properties for the skin.

You can absolutely make a pleasing scent with essential oils alone, but I recommend layering essential oils with fragrance oils at least a few times to see what you come up with. It really opens up the world of scent when you can mix and match herbaceous essential oils with notes that aren't available in this form, such as blackberry or musk.

Essential oils to avoid while pregnant

The use of essential oils during pregnancy is a sensitive topic, which is why I always include this part in all of my books. There are some who swear by certain essential oils for pregnancy, and some who believe you should avoid all of them until birth. It's very common for women to develop sensitivity to essential oils during pregnancy, even if you've used them for a long time. Opposite is a list of essential oils that are generally considered unsafe for pregnancy because they can cause contractions or other complications. However, keep in mind that everybody is different, so even if an oil is not on the list it doesn't mean you won't have a reaction to it during pregnancy. Stop using any essential oils immediately if they cause discomfort, and be sure to check with your doctor if you have any concerns about their safety.

aniseed	basil	birch	camphor
caraway	cassia	cedarwood/thuja	cinnamon
clary sage	clove	deertongue	fennel
hyssop	juniper berry	marjoram	mugwort
nutmeg	oregano	parsley	pennyroyal
rosemary	rue	sage	sassafras
tansy	tarragon	tonka	wintergreen
wormwood			

EXTRACTS

Extracts are generally alcohol based and can offer some fragrance to water-based formulas; however, they are most useful for introducing the energy of a plant that is either not readily available, too costly in essential oil form, or you wish to forgo using essential oils in favor of fragrance oils.

Many extracts are not oil soluble, which means they will not mix with the oil in your formulation. Most are water soluble and will dissolve completely into waters or liquids. Extracts are ideal when you'd like to infuse the energy of a plant that is only available as a vegetable oil, such as coconut, pecan, or pomegranate, or for essential oils that are very costly such as vanilla absolute. You can find a wide variety of extracts in specialty food stores or online.

Avoid imitation extracts that are made with chemical components, animal components, or other unknown materials.

You can make your own extracts by making tinctures. Tinctures are very easy to make, and can keep for years in some cases. See page 150 for a basic alcohol tincture recipe.

CARRIER OILS

Carrier oils are sometimes called base, fixed, or vegetable oils. They are created from a variety of plant materials such as nuts, seeds, fruits, and vegetables, as the latter name suggests. Just like essential oils, each carrier oil has a unique energetic frequency that can enhance or dilute the energy of your blends. Also like essential oils, they have healing properties that can contribute to any skin or body concerns you wish to address. Be sure to check out each chapter to see which carrier oils are right for your beauty intention or body concern.

CREAMS AND LOTIONS

Creams and lotions are an easy way to sneak in energetic or healing properties whether you wish to encourage more self-worth, for example, or treat really itchy skin. They're so easy to customize, especially if you use a lotion base. I have provided a cream recipe you can make from scratch for those wishing for more of a challenge, meaning you'll have to emulsify the wax and water content. Most of the recipes in this book utilize a lotion base, but you can also buy unscented lotion bases from Amazon.

Whether you choose to go the DIY route and make your creams from scratch or you use a base, adding healing ingredients is really quite easy. Tinctures and oils can be added in small amounts, about one teaspoon at a time. Just be sure to go slow so you don't destabilize the lotion: too much water or cream can cause the oils and water to separate. You can also add essential or fragrance oils to make your beauty potions more beautiful.

SALTS AND SUGARS

Salts and sugars are the perfect base for body and hair scrubs. While there are many different salts to choose from, for the purposes of this book I recommend sticking to sugar, salt, and Epsom salt. These three options will cover most of your needs. You can use a variety of salts such as red or pink salt if you like, but they aren't necessary and will just be an added expense.

WATER

As a rule of thumb, distilled water should be used for any preparations intended for the body and calls for water such as toners, teas, sprays, room sprays, and herbal infusions. Distilled water is created by boiling it into vapor, then condensing it back into liquid form. Doing so removes impurities and bacteria that could introduce mold and other harmful contaminants into your potions. Distilled water is inexpensive and easy to find in all major grocery stores.

HYDROSOLS AND FLORAL WATERS

Herbal distillates, more commonly known as hydrosols and floral waters, can be used in place of or in addition to distilled water. The most common and readily available ones are rose water, lavender water and orange blossom, but a hydrosol can be made with almost any plant material. Some of my favorites are jasmine, vetiver, cucumber, baked earth, and cypress, but you can find a wide variety of options online.

Hydrosols and floral waters are also distilled, which means any contaminants have been removed and are safe for use in body formulations. They contain small amounts of essential oil – usually 1 percent or less – from the plant material used to create them, giving them additional energetic and medicinal benefits. Though the amount of essential oil is small, you will find most hydrosols and floral waters are quite fragrant and can add an extra layer to both your potion's magic and the scent experience. Be sure to purchase them from a reputable source, as many commercialized hydrosols are actually distilled water with drops of essential or fragrance oil and so aren't the same as a hydrosol.

To correctly store hydrosols and floral waters, keep them in dark containers in the refrigerator if possible or at the least out of direct sunlight. Herbal distillates are highly volatile and can spoil very quickly at different rates. With proper care, most hydros and floral waters will last six to eight months. Throw away the water if it becomes cloudy or develops a smell, or if sediment begins to form.

ALCOHOLS AND WITCH HAZELS

I love adding alcohol to my sprays, as each one has a unique scent profile that can really enhance the other ingredients. Whiskey pairs well with woods and vanilla, brandy with sweeter fragrances and florals, while vodka is perfect for fresh and bright blends and gin for juniper, of course. Not only do they add complexity to your fragrance, but they serve a practical use as well. Alcohol helps to prevent bacteria growth and can extend the shelf life of your formulas, and they can also be infused with plant material that is not readily available in essential oil form, adding one more layer of intention and magic. Try infusing alcohol with unusual ingredients such as moss, fruits, vegetables, vanilla beans, and resins.

Commercially prepared witch hazel can be used to add an astringent quality to water-based formulas. It isn't as powerful as alcohol for reducing bacteria, but it makes a gentle toner for beauty remedies. You can also create a witch hazel tincture by infusing witch hazel bark into alcohol, following the basic tincture recipe on page 150, though unlike the commercial version a home-made witch hazel tincture will create a brownish liquid and take on the smell of the alcohol used.

PART II

NURTURING INNER BEAUTY

I truly believe beauty begins within and, even more specifically than that, beauty begins with the mind. How you see yourself is going to have a direct impact on how you carry yourself and, thus, how others perceive you. If you go through the world with confidence and a strong sense of self-worth, then that light you carry within you will shine for the rest of the world to see. It almost doesn't matter what your beauty routine looks like if your inner world is constantly plagued with doubt and insecurities: you'll never glow quite as much as you would when you have a strong attitude toward yourself.

CHAPTER 3

A BEAUTIFUL MIND

A beautiful life starts with a beautiful mindset. How you view yourself and the world around you has a huge impact on how you perceive beauty. Generally, if you're a positive person you're more likely to find beauty in everyday experiences, even ones that aren't so enjoyable. However, if you tend to be more negative then you'll likely be someone who finds it challenging to see the world with a sense of wonder and awe.

Beyond that, having a beautiful mindset means understanding your idea of what beauty actually is, rather than allowing yourself to be influenced by others who perhaps do not share your values. That's why in this chapter you'll excavate your mind to discover what beauty means to you, but I do challenge you to look deeper rather than jumping to conclusions. Instead of focusing on skin-deep things such as full hair or radiant skin, turn your attention to things such as a confident smile, letting your natural beauty shine through rather than covering it up, or finding beauty in an imperfect piece of décor, artwork, or clothing. At the same time, if you're high maintenance in any part of your life then that's also okay. I'll tell you a secret: I'm a high-maintenance girly. There . . . I said it!

For a long time I didn't allow myself to be like that because I work in the spiritual and wellness industry, where it isn't uncommon to find people in mumus or yoga pants, wearing very minimal makeup if any at all, and filling their homes with boho chic décor. None of that is me. I worked in fashion before my time in the spiritual world, so a beautiful aesthetic in my mind is high but classic fashion, traditional décor (hello, British country homes) and mixed prints in a minimal color palette, chic makeup and hair, and more classic artforms. However, because of my work I felt obligated to wear what others wore or adjust my style to fit what was trending in the industry. I stopped wearing makeup, styling my hair and wearing designer clothes for years to fit in, and all the while parts of me slowly shrunk and died.

I know what it's like to not feel beautiful because I didn't feel true to myself, which of course means I'm not here to tell you to change your idea of what beautiful means for you. It doesn't matter if you're high maintenance, low maintenance or somewhere in between: this is about what beauty means to you and nothing else.

In this chapter you'll find a selection of journal prompts, exercises, rituals, and recipes to help you dive deep into your brain, creating your version of beauty. My intention is for you to end up with a set of values or feelings that will help you understand your idea of beauty, and not just when it comes to how you look. The principles that define your idea of beauty apply to all areas of your life, whether that's your home or relationships or your next plate of food.

TAKING STOCK OF YOUR BEAUTIFUL MIND: AN EXERCISE IN SELF-AWARENESS

Grab a pen and several pieces of paper or a journal, preferably in a style that feels pretty to you, and work your way through the following journal prompts. Take your time with these, as your answers to the questions are going to open up a lot of untended spaces in your spirit. Tough feelings might come up, or the need to confront mistruths you've carried for a long time. There's no rush here: you can take as long as you need, even years, to go through the questions.

I would also recommend coming back to the questions over time, as your idea of beauty can evolve. For a long time my favorite colors were beige and grey when beauty to me felt very minimal. Now, as I write this book, my favorite colors have grown to be shades of merlot and plum. It might be something else a year from now, and I welcome that with open arms. Humans are complex, and what we believe is beautiful will be complex as well.

Definition of beauty

- What are the first things that come to mind when you think of the word "beauty"?
- How would you define something that is beautiful?
- How would you define a beautiful person?
- What does inner beauty mean to you?
- What does natural beauty mean to you?
- Is there anything about your definition of beauty that feels like it's based on external factors or pressures?
- If so, do you consider these definitions to be a healthy expression of *your* beauty?

Personal beauty

- Do you fit your definition of beauty?
- If not, how are you different from your definition of beauty?
- Do you believe you're beautiful?
- What's the most beautiful thing about you?
- What, if anything, do you believe makes you less than beautiful?
- Why aren't these things attractive to you?
- How would you change them if you could?
- How do you express your idea of beauty?
- What do you do to enhance your beauty?

A beautiful history

- What do others find beautiful about you?
- What kind of people do you find to be beautiful? Describe them in full detail.
- What's beautiful about your heritage or culture?
- Do you have any family members, traditions, or experiences that represent beauty for you?

Beautiful growth

- What expectations of beauty have you struggled to let go of?
- In what ways have your family, culture, or society influenced your idea of what is beautiful?
- What's a challenge or obstacle you've faced that ultimately brought you a more beautiful understanding of life?
- What's beautiful about humanity?

Everyday beauty

- What are the most beautiful colors?
- What are the most beautiful textures and patterns?
- What is the most beautiful part about the place where you live?
- Who are the most beautiful people in your life?
- What is the most beautiful thing about your day?
- If you were living your sense of beauty, what would a day in your life look like?

THE THREE "SELF-" PRINCIPLES OF A BEAUTIFUL MIND

Self-awareness

Self-awareness is the foundation of any personal evolution, be it beauty, abundance, confidence, or healing. Knowing what you need is how you gather information that tells you where to start and where to go from there. If ever you're feeling confused, start with where you are and take inventory of how you feel and how you'd like to feel. Do so with as much honesty as you can. Don't worry about "should feel" or "should desire": approaching self-awareness from the lens of "should" only muddies the water.

Practice self-awareness: create a list of things you do regularly, beauty or otherwise. Focus on things that are within your control such as which makeup colors you wear, the types of coffee you drink, movies you watch and so on. Go through each thing on this list and ask yourself: "Does this still feel like me?"

Self-identify

Self-awareness leads to self-identity. It's so much easier to be influenced by external forces when you don't have a sense of what you value and need to feel whole. Knowing your needs, desires, motivations, and what you wish to avoid is a recipe for knowing who you really are and gives you the ammunition needed to say "No" to anything that isn't in alignment with you. It also gives you the clarity to say Yes," to know when something truly lights you up. However, it's important to understand that identity is something that isn't stationary. Yours will evolve, shift, and sometimes completely reinvent itself and that's perfectly okay. In fact, it's quite beautiful. Knowing you have permission to grow gives you the space to try out new things or perhaps revisit things that weren't right for you in the past but feel more resonant now.

Practice self-identity: knowing where a desire or need comes from can help you better sort what is a part of your true identity or something you've picked up along the way. Whenever a desire or urge to do something comes up, take the time to stop and ask yourself: "Where does this desire come from and does it truly belong to me?" Keep in mind that it's totally fine to want something that didn't originate from you as long as it's a conscious choice. This exercise isn't about denying yourself anything; rather, it's a chance to make deliberate choices for yourself that are in alignment with who you really are.

Self-confidence

Self-confidence begins with belief in yourself, in trusting yourself to know you can do hard things, that you can fail and bounce back or that you are beautiful in your own ways. To be self-confident is to cherish your inner light without apology, to shine even when others say you shouldn't. It's challenging to feel confident when you've been taught to be humble or avoid standing out. Know that you can be humble, yet puff out your chest: one need not rule out the other.

Practice self-confidence: create a confidence log. Every day or so write down one thing you did successfully or that made you feel proud of yourself. This can be things such as a problem you figured out, something you were complimented on, an outfit you put together and really loved, a task you did really well, or a brilliant idea. Take a few moments to review previous entries whenever you add a new one and watch as all the beautiful things you've done start to add up.

Beautiful mind allies

Below is a list of ingredients that align with the three principles of a beautiful mind: self- awareness, self-identity, and self-confidence. Consider the items on the list when making your own beautiful apothecary recipes. You can brew them as teas, make tinctures to use in sprays or baths, or top candles to infuse them with the plant's energy. You can also bring the energy of these principles into your personal space, such as on a beauty altar (page 144) or as décor pieces.

Please note, however, that not all herbs and flowers are suitable for ingesting and/or they may interfere with some medications. Remember, also, that it is not advisable to ingest essential oils. Be sure to speak with a qualified health-care professional before using anything internally.

BEAUTIFUL MIND PRINCIPLE	ESSENTIAL OILS	PLANTS	CARRIER OILS
Self-awareness	Anise, clary sage, cypress, fir, frankincense, labdanum, lavender, mugwort, nutmeg, petitgrain, pine, rosemary, sage, spearmint, valerian	Citronella, orris root, peppermint, poppy seeds, primrose	Almond, borage, camellia, grape, sunflower
Self-identity	Amyris, bay, cajeput, cananga, cassia, cedar, celery, clary sage, cypress, fennel, fir, geranium, litsea, neroli, orange, rose, tea tree	Carnation, citronella, fennel, ginkgo, horehound, mistletoe, vervain, violet	Camellia, grape, jojoba, sunflower
Self-confidence	Basil, bergamot, cardamom, cedar, geranium, jasmine, lemon, petitgrain, pine, rose, tea tree, yarrow	Cedar, celandine, cinquefoil, ginger, high John, honeysuckle, motherwort, neroli, yarrow	Borage, camellia, rosehip, sunflower

Retreat: Herbal Bathing Salts for Contemplation and Soul Work

These salts feel most at home during the winter season, but they can be used at any time for clarity, contemplation, realigning to your purpose, and gaining new perspective. They are crafted with essential oils that are known for their ability to restore peace, encourage well-being, and bring your soul back to joy. I love to soak in them just before reflecting or answering journal prompts such as the beautiful mind prompts on page 77.

- 10 drops of cypress essential oil
- 10 drops of bergamot essential oil
- 10 drops of lavender essential oil
- 1 cup Epsom or solar salts
- ½ cup sea salt
- ½ tsp rosemary powder
- ½ tsp oat straw powder
- ½ tsp peppermint powder

Mix the essential oils together in a small bowl and set aside. Combine the salts and herbal powders, then slowly add the essential oil mixture to the salt mixture while stirring with a spoon to distribute the essential oil.

To use, add the desired amount to a warm bath and soak for about 20 minutes. If desired, bathe with a piece of clear quartz crystal. While soaking, ask your soul to show you what it needs to see most and contemplate on the answers you receive. Store the remaining bathing salts in a container with a tight-fitting lid.

A BEAUTIFUL MIND BATH AND BODY OIL

I made this oil to encourage gratitude and an overall positive outlook on life. Gratitude takes a lot of self-awareness: you have to be able to reflect on the good in your life in order to express gratitude for it. It can seem daunting or as though you have one more thing on the to-do list to keep a gratitude journal; I get that. I do recommend keeping a gratitude journal, but even if you can't it's pretty easy to work gratitude into your day with a little bit of intention. Use this oil as you would you regular body oil, and while you massage it into your skin say one to three things you're grateful for.

- dried flowers*, optional
- 76 drops of lavender essential oil
- 72 drops of bergamot essential oil
- 32 drops of Bulgarian rose essential oil (or other rose essential oil)
- 20 drops of clove essential oil
- 1 vitamin E capsule
- 2 oz | 60 ml shea or rosehip oil
- 2 oz | 60 ml watermelon seed oil

Slip any flowers or herbs into a small bottle, then add the combined essential oils mixture. Prick the vitamin E capsule with a needle and squeeze the contents into the bottle, then fill the bottle with the shea and watermelon seed oils. Cap and shake well. Hold the bottle in your hands and bring it to your heart. Dedicate this bottle to the feeling of gratitude with a short prayer of your choice. You might say something like "The contents of this bottle always bring more things for me to be grateful for." Follow your prayer with a closing statement such as "Amen" or "So it is."

Use your body oil as you would any other body oil by massaging it into very slightly damp skin after a warm bath or shower. Add a teaspoon to a warm bath for a skin-softening self-care treatment, or massage a few drops into your scalp and on the ends of your hair for daily conditioning.

* I recently dried a bouquet of hydrangea flowers that ended up being a beautiful dusty rose color and felt like the epitome of gratitude, so I slipped those into the bottle along with some lavender buds and an autumn-colored foliage leaf. Gratitude, for me at least, brings to mind softness, beauty, and harmony, so having dried flowers felt like a natural fit. Feel free to omit them or swap them out with other flowers and herbs of your choice.

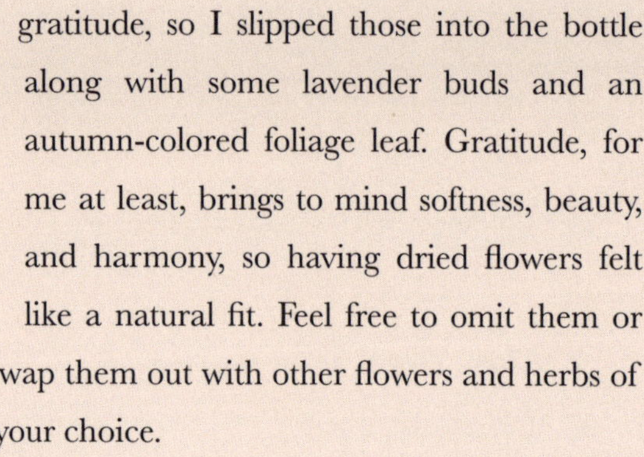

Self-confidence spray

Here's another little secret: I doubt myself a lot and have to work very hard to believe in myself and what I can accomplish. I'm always second-guessing myself, especially when it comes to writing my books and decks. Are people going to like this? Is what I'm writing stupid? Does it even make sense?

I keep this confidence spray near my desk, so when my thoughts are spinning I can grab it, spray it a few times, and stop the defeating self-talk in its tracks.

- 4 oz | 120 ml water
- 7 drops of basil essential oil
- 2 drops of peppermint essential oil
- 2 drops of jasmine absolute
- 9 drops of palma rosa essential oil
- 1 tsp peppermint tincture or mint water

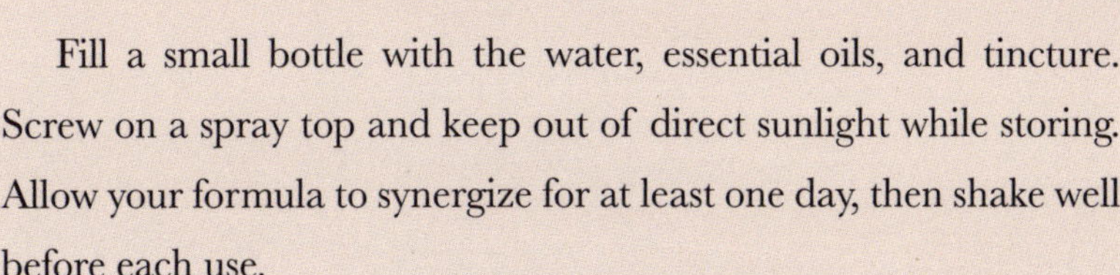

Fill a small bottle with the water, essential oils, and tincture. Screw on a spray top and keep out of direct sunlight while storing. Allow your formula to synergize for at least one day, then shake well before each use.

To use, shake well, spray a few times and repeat: "I will not give into self-defeating thoughts and feelings." The spray will stay fresh for up to 12 months.

Follow Your Passions Bath Salts

Building a self-identity requires one main thing: following your passions. What you're passionate about is useful information, letting you know the things that bring energy and joy to your spirit. These bath salts are meant to help you find creative outlets and ways to express your identity. It's a bit different from self-expression, as these salts are about opening the door to possibilities and helping you to discover what makes you, you.

- 1 cup salt of your choice
- ½ cup Epsom salt
- ½ cup baking soda
- 2 tbs rose petal powder
- 1 tsp dried orange peel
- ½ tsp cinnamon powder
- 1 tsp vanilla extract

Mix the dry ingredients in a bowl, then add the vanilla extract and stir well. To use, add to a warm bath and soak for 20 to 30 minutes. While relaxing, close your eyes and ask the spirit of Aries to show you what your true passions are or to show you something about your true nature.

SPIRIT OINTMENT TO UPLIGHT ENERGY

Having an ointment in your bag or around your space whenever you want a quick energetic pick me up is never a bad idea. I keep one in my car to use after events: I love doing live events, but meeting so many people at one time can be really draining. I've tried it a few times already and it really makes a difference and restores my energy.

- 1 cup sunflower oil
- 1 tbs dried hyssop
- 1 tbs dried peppermint

Add the oil and herbs to a glass measuring cup, and sit the cup in a saucepan with a few inches of water over low heat. You can also add to a glass heat-proof teapot and warm gently over low heat for 10 to 20 minutes. Remove from the heat and allow the herbs to steep until the mixture is cooled to room temperature. Strain the herbs and store in a dark bottle.

FOR THE OINTMENT:

- ¼ cup hyssop/peppermint–infused sunflower oil
- 1 tbs beeswax or vegan wax of choice
- few drops of vitamin E oil
- 20 drops of amyris essential oil
- 6 drops of lime essential oil
- 2 drops of angelica root essential oil
- 1 drop of bergamot essential oil

Add the infused oil and beeswax to a clean measuring cup, and sit the cup in a saucepan with a few inches of water over low heat until melted. Remove from the heat, add the vitamin E oil and essential oils and mix well. Pour the oil mixture into a small tin or pot and allow it to cool and harden completely before use. Rub a little bit of the ointment on the backs of hands, the inside of your wrists, and along your collarbone to restore vitality and lift vibrations.

CHAPTER 4

A BEAUTIFUL HEART

I believe a beautiful heart begins with loving yourself. It's very hard to open your heart when you've convinced yourself that you aren't lovable or that you aren't valuable. It's even more challenging to radiate beauty when you're putting yourself down. People respond to the energy you send out into the world, and the energy you send out into the world is a reflection of how you feel on the inside, which includes how you feel about yourself.

When it comes to cultivating a beautiful heart, you could spend a lot of time doing elaborate workshops or going on an intense retreat, but I think the easiest and most effective way to facilitate self-love is just by setting aside some time for yourself. I know you've probably heard a million times that self-care isn't just about baths, but you know what: sometimes it's exactly that. Sometimes all you need is 30 minutes to yourself to say "My self-care matters."

In this chapter we'll focus on beauty remedies that are pretty and indulgent but energetically open your heart, allowing you to rediscover your sense of worth so you can fall back in love with yourself. The ritual provided in this chapter isn't meant to take the entire day because I get it: you have a lot of things going on. The idea of an entire self-care day sounds amazing, but if all you can afford right now is a morning then let that be enough. A beautiful heart is about quality, not quantity.

THE THREE "SELF-" PRINCIPLES OF A BEAUTIFUL HEART

Self-compassion

Offer yourself some grace, my darling. We all make mistakes and we all have things we wish we could've done differently. We all have things we wish we could be better at, or things we just can't seem to get right. Don't beat yourself up for anything: not for being tired or needing a break, not for not being unable to do more with your day, not for failing at a goal or disappointing someone. Instead, offer yourself some forgiveness and permission to move on but, more than that, remember that you're human. This means you aren't going to get it right all of the time. This isn't a unique problem to you: it's the human experience, and you shouldn't suffer for it any more than anyone else.

Practice self-compassion: write down everything you feel you've done wrong or every way you feel you've fallen short as though you're writing to a friend asking for advice. Respond to the letter like you would respond to anyone you care about. What would you say? How would you offer compassion for them? What would you tell them to do next to heal and move on? Answer as objectively as you can. Repeat this exercise whenever you're frustrated with yourself about something and need to show yourself some grace.

Self-worth

To have self-worth means you see yourself as having value, which in turn means you matter and you are deserving of a great, beautiful life. It also means you celebrate the things you've done well. I really dislike the practice of being humble, not because there's anything wrong with humility but because when you're told to be humble you're essentially being told to subdue yourself. It also means you shouldn't express pride in yourself for doing a great job or that you shouldn't state matter of factly that, yes, you are really good at something. Over time, most of us have learned to play down our accomplishments rather than fully celebrating them, but celebrating yourself doesn't need to be grand or even shared with others. It's merely an act of self-love and a reminder that you have plenty of worth.

Practice self-worth: clap for yourself at least once a day. Find something in your day you feel proud of, even if it's something small. It could be not going over budget while shopping or going out of your way to help someone. When you find something that makes you feel proud or indicates you've done a good job, give yourself a big round of applause. Physically put your hands together and clap to celebrate yourself.

Self-trust

To have self-trust means you believe in yourself. I think this is an important step in the journey toward having a beautiful heart, because if you don't believe in yourself how can anyone else believe in you? To build self-trust you must be willing to honor your commitments, which of course means knowing how much you can realistically handle. A lot of regret comes from missing being honest about your needs, so that when you take on something you know you can take it seriously and commit to it.

Practice self-trust: make a to-do list at the beginning of each week. Write down everything you wish to do for the week, and once you're done cut that list in half. Celebrate every time you accomplish something on your list that represents you keeping your word to yourself. At the end of the week, reflect on how much of the list you've accomplished.

BEAUTIFUL HEART ALLIES

Below is a list of ingredients that align with the three principles of a beautiful heart: self-compassion, self-worth, and self-trust. Consider the items on this list when making your own beautiful apothecary recipes. You can brew them as teas, make tinctures to use in sprays or baths, or top candles to infuse them with the plant's energy. You can also bring the energy of these principles into your personal space, such as on a beauty altar (see page 144) or as décor pieces.

Please note, however, that not all herbs and flowers are suitable for ingesting and/or may interfere with some medications. Remember, also, that it is not advisable to ingest essential oils. Be sure to speak with a qualified health-care professional before using anything internally.

BEAUTIFUL HEART PRINCIPLE	ESSENTIAL OILS	PLANTS	CARRIER OILS
Self-compassion	Amyris, angelica, bergamot, grapefruit, lavender, lemon, lime, mandarin, marjoram, neroli, parsley, peppermint, valerian, yarrow	Basil, burdock, cypress, hawthorn, milk thistle, peony, rose, sugar cane, tarragon, violet	Almond, apricot, evening primrose, flax, grape, rosehip
Self-worth	Amyris, angelica, bergamot, cananga, catnip, chamomile, coriander, geranium, jasmine, litsea, myrtle, neroli, orange, palma rosa, rose, tagetes, tarragon	Barberry, burdock, cedar, chervil, heliotrope, lovage, marigold, sage	Avocado, camellia, jojoba, olive, sunflower
Self-trust	Amyris, basil, birch, clary sage, geranium, helichrysum, labdanum, lemon balm, lemongrass, neroli, pine, rose, spearmint, spruce, valerian, ylang ylang	Butterbur, calamint, frangipani, iris, mustard seed, neroli, rose (especially pink shades), rue, sage	Borage, grape, rosehip, sunflower

Self-centered: a ritual for a beautiful morning of falling back in love with yourself

Taking care of myself doesn't mean "me first." It means "me too."

– L.R. KNOSTS

It's okay to take the morning to be self-centered, but it's better if you can take an entire day. I don't mean the kind of self-centeredness that makes you selfish or self-absorbed. What I mean is focusing on *your* needs, desires, growth, and self-care. It's a concept that's taken me years to learn. How can you find a life you love living if you're too tired, stressed, and distracted? Well, it's going to be a real challenge, that's for sure.

Setting aside one day a week for an indulgent day is just the ticket to restore your energy, and if you can't commit to one day a week then try one day every fortnight or once a month. As long as it happens on a regular basis and you make it a priority then you are well on your way to bringing more beauty and thus personal care into your life. Try this ritual:

- Start the morning with a glass of Venusian beauty water (page 103) to rehydrate. You can add a dash of salt or hydration drops for extra hydration.
- Do a light stretch or yoga routine to unlock stiff muscles from the night before.

- Light candles with a pleasing scent to fill your home with a beautiful fragrance. Be sure to add several to the bathroom before moving on to the next step. The veil of Venus candle on page 104 is especially lovely for a day like this.
- Prepare a hot bath to have ready once you're done with the next step, allowing your bath to cool to a comfortable temperature.
- Spend a solid 10 minutes or more gently scrubbing the self-consecration body scrub (page 106) over your entire body, focusing on the places that tend to be neglected such as your knees, elbows, feet, the back of your neck, and behind your ears and jaws.
- Add 1 to 2 tablespoons or as much as you like of the indulgent self-love bath elixir (page 108) to the bath water and soak for 20 minutes. Keep a glass of Venusian beauty water (opposite) nearby to sip while soaking.
- Towel yourself dry but leave your skin just a little moist, and massage sacred body oil for self-love (page 110) into your skin.
- Finish off with a few dabs of self-devotion perfume (page 132). Apply it to the backs of your knees, your neck, behind your ears, and along your chest and under your arms for a long-lasting fragrance.

Venusian Beauty Water

This tea is jam-packed with vitamin C and other nutrients that are not only amazing for beauty, but for overall well-being. These herbs steep well in the refrigerator overnight, especially hibiscus. Since Venus corresponds to Friday, I like to make up a jar every Thursday night to sip throughout the next day. I also love to enjoy it on my self-care days to stay hydrated while enjoying a nourishing bath. You can omit the honey but be warned: this can be a little tart without it.

- 1 tsp dried rosehips
- ½ tsp dried rose petals
- ½ tsp dried hibiscus leaves
- cold water
- 1 rose quartz crystal
- honey to taste, optional

Add all of the ingredients to a mason jar and shake well. Allow the mixture to steep in the refrigerator overnight, then strain out the herbs and rose quartz and enjoy. You can also drink the water immediately if you prefer a milder taste.

Note: I'm not going to lie, I eyeball the herbs most of the time but I have provided measurements to give you a general rule of thumb.

Veil of Venus Candle

Libra is the zodiac sign of beauty, so I had to include at least a few things with Venus energy. The dried florals really make this candle, and I highly recommend drying your own flowers if you can. I've been using a selection of dried roses, amaranth, yarrow, lisianthus and carnations in shades of dark pink, deep reds, and greens. I like to make a variety of different sizes to cluster together when I want to add a pretty touch around the house, especially for self-care days.

- a candle-making kit
- 1 oz | 30 ml blend of essential oils (equal parts jasmine, neroli and geranium) or floral fragrance oil
- optional toppings: a variety of dried flowers

As with all candles in this book you can definitely buy all of the ingredients separately to make candles, but if you're a beginner or don't see yourself making boxes of candles I recommend starting with a kit. It will have everything you need to make several candles at the most economical price.

Begin by weighing the wax in the kit. You can do so using the container to scoop up the wax, using two scoops for each container.

Add the wax to the pitcher included in the kit and place it on the wax melter. Alternatively, you can place the pitcher inside a pot of water and set it on the stove. Stir with a silicone spatula to help the wax melt. Once it is completely melted, stir in 1 oz | 30 ml of essential oil for every 16 oz | 475 ml of wax, which will make two 8 oz | 250 g candles. Be sure to stir well for 2 to 3 minutes to ensure the wax and essential oils bind correctly, otherwise the fragrance may later separate from the wax.

Put the wick sticker included in the kit on the bottom of the metal foot attached to the wick. Pull the paper off the other side of the stick and do your best to place the wick in the center of the jar. Use the metal centering tool included in the kit to hold the wick steady. Repeat until you have wicked all of the candle jars.

Of course, you do not need to use the jars included in the kit; however, not all jars or containers are well suited for candles and especially not glass, which can shatter at high temperatures. If you're using glass, choose a thicker option or consider a metal tin.

Pour the wax into the jar and recenter the wick if necessary. Allow the candles to cool for several hours. I recommend arranging your items on a cold candle before melting the wax so you can move things around and decide on the look you're going for. The wax will dry quickly and you may not be able to move things around once you place them, similar to the experience of using a hot glue gun. Start with the larger items first, then add smaller items to fill in the gaps.

When you've decided on the placement of your toppings, gently melt the top layer of wax using a hair dryer or heat gun. You only need about ⅛ in | 3 mm of melted wax on top: any more than that and the toppings will sink in and won't show on top. Sprinkle the dried toppings in your desired pattern and let the wax harden again.

Trim the wick to ¼ in | 6.5 mm. Let the candles rest for at least another 24 to 72 hours before burning, because the longer you let them cure the stronger the fragrance will be and the harder the wax will become. A harder wax means it takes less time for the candle to burn down completely, prolonging the life of the candle.

To burn, place the candle on a heat-proof surface and light it, burning for a full four hours. It's important to do this on your first burn to avoid tunneling (when a candle burns mostly at the center, leaving unburned wax at the edges).

Self-Consecration Body Scrub

"Consecration" is defined as the action of making or declaring something sacred. It's a ritualistic process of committing to a goal or idea and leaving behind all things that distract you from your mission. Scrubs are a great way to represent this process. Scrub away the energy that doesn't serve you while letting the fragrance and healing almond oil nourish your skin and renew your vitality, supporting you in your desired outcome.

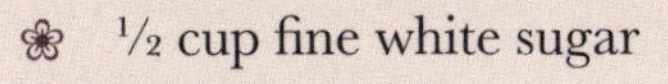

- ½ cup fine white sugar
- ½ cup pink salt
- 1 tsp rose powder
- ¼ cup almond oil
- 1 tbs melted shea butter
- 1 vitamin E capsule
- 30 drops of rose absolute oil
- 12 drops of peppermint essential oil

Whisk together the sugar, salt and rose powder in a bowl. Using a heavy spoon, combine the dry mixture with the remaining ingredients until well combined. Spoon into a container with a tight lid and store in a cool, dark place; refrigeration is not required. To apply, massage a small amount onto moist skin, rubbing in a counterclockwise motion. Rinse. Use within six to eight months.

State out loud: *"I vow to release the experiences and people who enslave my soul to low vibrations, chaos, and self-destruction. I give myself permission to heal and move on."*

Indulgent Self-Love Bath Elixir

I've been making bathing elixirs and cordials for years. I stumbled across a similar recipe in a very old book, and I'm still surprised you don't see them more often. I suppose it's because alcohol can be expensive, but some discount alcohol retailers sell cheap bottles of hard spirits. In fact, I bought a bottle of same-brand rum for $6, and as you'll see from the recipe that one bottle can go a very long way.

Why use alcohol? It's a non-abrasive exfoliant although it shouldn't be confused for rubbing alcohol, which dries out the skin. Hibiscus is an equally underrated but wonderful ingredient. It contains a substance called mucilage, which is incredibly moisturizing paired with its vitamin C content, making it a lush treat for skin. Of course, all of the ingredients featured here have energetic benefits that align with the energy of love and self-care.

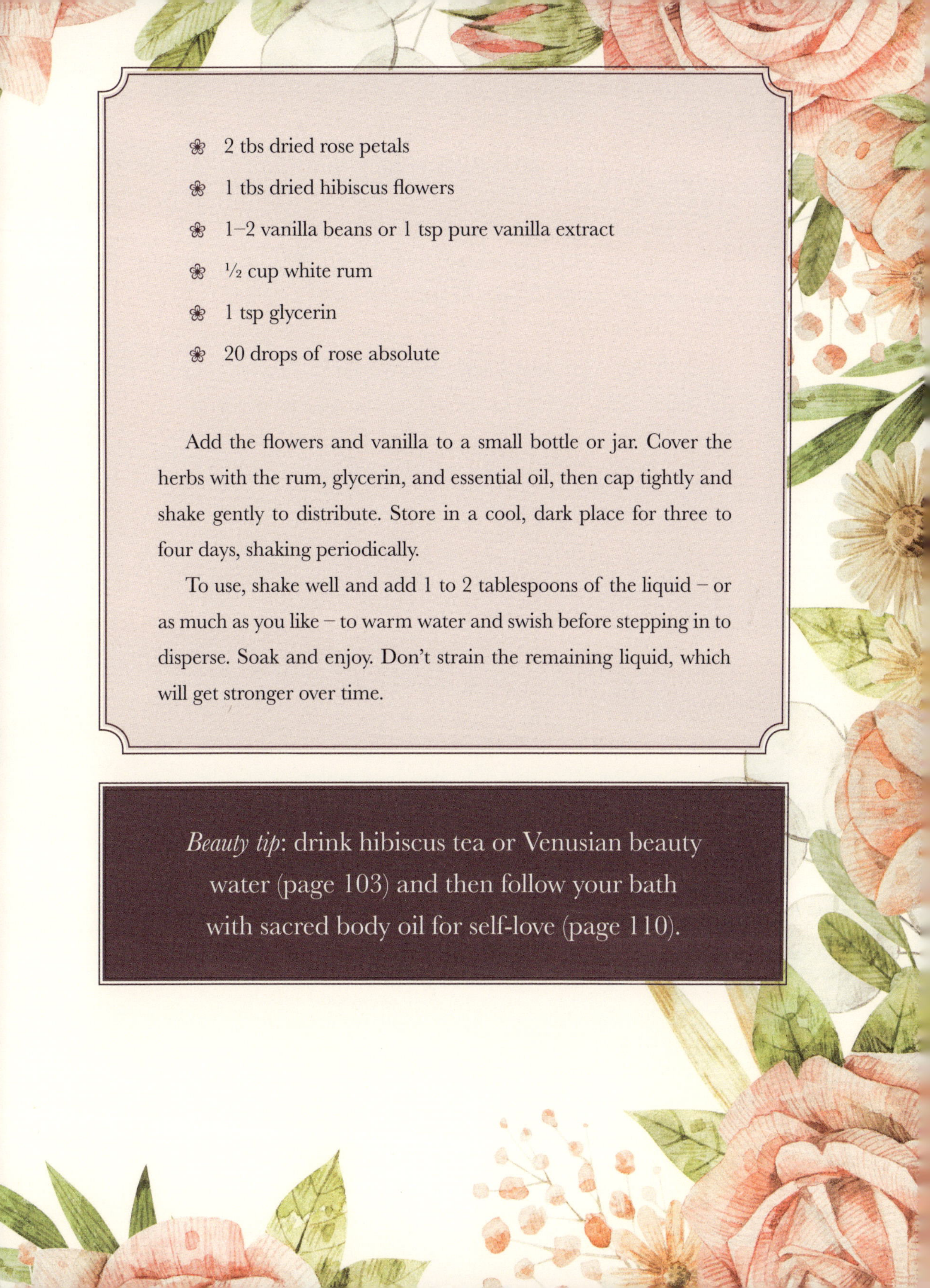

- 2 tbs dried rose petals
- 1 tbs dried hibiscus flowers
- 1–2 vanilla beans or 1 tsp pure vanilla extract
- ½ cup white rum
- 1 tsp glycerin
- 20 drops of rose absolute

Add the flowers and vanilla to a small bottle or jar. Cover the herbs with the rum, glycerin, and essential oil, then cap tightly and shake gently to distribute. Store in a cool, dark place for three to four days, shaking periodically.

To use, shake well and add 1 to 2 tablespoons of the liquid – or as much as you like – to warm water and swish before stepping in to disperse. Soak and enjoy. Don't strain the remaining liquid, which will get stronger over time.

Beauty tip: drink hibiscus tea or Venusian beauty water (page 103) and then follow your bath with sacred body oil for self-love (page 110).

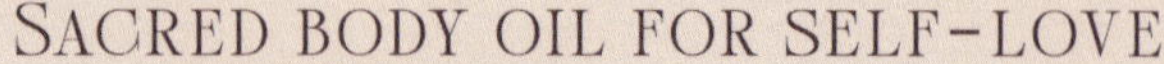

Sacred Body Oil for Self-Love

You are a sacred being, and I want you to have an oil that embodies the energy of self-care, self-compassion, and self-love. This oil was made specifically for people who are ready to focus on loving themselves. Watermelon seed can be a little challenging to find but it is available online, and I highly recommend it. It's so soothing to the skin and has such a soft energy, and because it's a little more unusual than your traditional carrier oil it feels very luxurious.

- 24 drops of vanilla absolute
- 18 drops of neroli essential oil
- 1 drop of geranium essential oil
- 2 oz | 60 ml watermelon seed oil or almond oil
- 1 vitamin E capsule

Add the combined essential oils to a small bottle. Prick the vitamin E capsule with a needle and squeeze the contents into the bottle. Fill the bottle with the watermelon or almond oil or a combination of both. Cap the bottle and shake it well. Place the bottle on your altar to synergize for at least 24 hours, then use as you would a traditional bath and body oil or to adorn ritual tools and candles.

CHAPTER 5

A BEAUTIFUL SOUL

When I think of a beautiful soul I think of someone who embodies the qualities of an angel: someone at peace who is light but also grounded; someone who fully shines and takes up space but also allows others to do the same. I believe you achieve these qualities by focusing on your own spiritual well-being, by taking time to tend to your soul's needs of protection, restoration, expression, and rest.

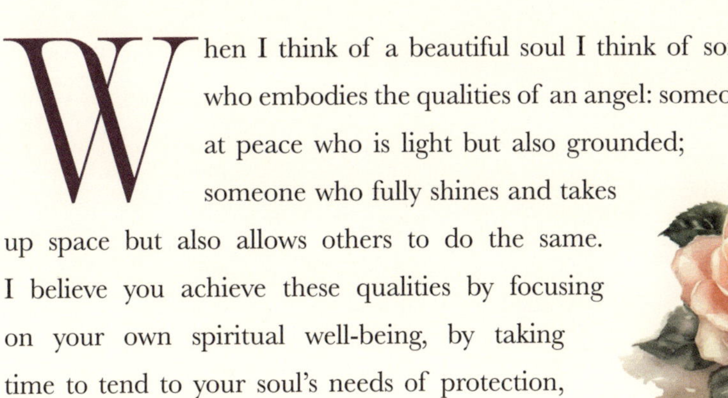

In this chapter I've included beauty remedies for bringing peace back to your soul. We tend to think of spiritual remedies and rituals as working with the moon or feminine energy, and while powerful these are not the only ways to revive your spirit. Simple and daily rituals can go a long way toward helping you find a state of calm and ease, or what I prefer to call "self-serenity," and all of the things in this chapter contribute to a feeling of self-devotion. To be devoted simply means to be loyal and loving to a person or cause, in this case you. When you show up to your regular soul rituals you are confirming your self-devotion. No additional steps.

Finally, this chapter covers self-expression. In my experience it's very challenging to express yourself fully when your soul feels depleted. Stress robs you of your ability to be true and kind to yourself and worry colors your vision with fears and insecurities that hold you back rather than lift you up, but once you find yourself in a state of self-serenity and self-devotion your soul will open up and self-expression will begin to blossom.

THE THREE "SELF-" PRINCIPLES OF A BEAUTIFUL SOUL

Self-serenity

Self-serenity is a fancy way of saying peace of mind. If you were to ask me what my definition of beauty is, one of the ways I would describe it is having peace. The ability to be calm and to know that everything is going to be okay is a beautiful thing indeed, and it makes life a little easier to manage when you've mastered peace. It also makes it easier to find beauty in the everyday. When your mind is packed with chaos and stress, it becomes challenging to allow yourself to find joy in your experiences. Cultivating peace opens your mind and soul to all of the wonderful things happening around you, regardless of how challenging today might feel.

Practice self-serenity: try practicing conscious breathing the next time you're feeling stressed. Close your eyes and listen to yourself breathe, following your breaths from start to end. Don't do anything else but sit and breathe. You don't have to do this for a long time; even a minute or two is helpful. Personally, I like to breathe in through the nose and out through the mouth, but breathing in and out through the nose is also okay.

After you've practiced breath awareness for a while you'll be ready to move up to following your breaths. Start by taking in a deep, full breath, about 80 percent of what you believe your lung capacity to be. Hold it for a few seconds, then exhale until you feel like your lungs are empty.

Being conscious of how much air you're taking in and how much air is going out is instantly calming and helps bring your mind to the present moment. You'll find it almost impossible to focus on anything else, restoring your state of mind to one of peace.

Self-expression

Self-expression is how you express your idea of beauty in the world. Remember that your specific version of beauty is a mirror of your soul, representing a part of who you are and what you find valuable or aesthetically pleasing. Everything about your life is an expression of your soul, from the clothes you wear to the types of foods you eat to the people you surround yourself with. I truly believe self-expression is the most spiritual thing you can do and also one of the purest things. To have a beautiful soul is to share that soul with others so they can also experience your inner beauty.

Practice self-expression: choose something quirky or unusual to carry with you every day. It can be a specific pen or perhaps a bag in a bold color or pattern, or maybe you'll wear a brooch every day. It can also be something non-physical such as a particular saying, or words you say often such as "Hello, darling." Commit to carrying or doing this thing every day for 30 days. With time, others will see or hear it and immediately associate it with you. They might see a bold bag one day and think "Oh, that's so like Jackie," or hear someone saying a vintage saying and think "Gosh, that makes me think of Violet."

Self-devotion

To be self-devoted means to be loyal to yourself. That can manifest in a variety of ways, from paying attention to your needs such as noticing when you're tired, frustrated or burnt out. It can also mean committing to your self-expression or moving through the world with confidence. Self-devotion is the last of the self principles because it's what happens when you embrace all other self principles. When you're aware, have a strong sense of identity, and have compassion you are taking steps to be more self-devoted.

Practice self-devotion: create a daily devotional practice with something that inspires you and motivates you. You may pull a daily card from an oracle deck that is especially comforting to you, watch an inspirational speech every morning that fires you up, or say a daily affirmation that fosters confidence.

BEAUTIFUL SOUL ALLIES

Below is a list of ingredients that align with the three principles of a beautiful soul: self-serenity, self-expression, and self-devotion. Consider the items on this list when making your own beautiful apothecary recipes. You can brew them as teas, make tinctures to use in sprays or baths, or top candles to infuse them with the plant's energy. You can also bring the energy of these principles into your personal space, such as on a beauty altar (see page 144) or as décor pieces.

Please note, however, that not all herbs and flowers are suitable for ingesting and/or may interfere with some medications. Remember, also, that it is not advisable to ingest essential oils. Be sure to speak with a qualified healthcare professional before using anything internally.

BEAUTIFUL SOUL PRINCIPLE	ESSENTIAL OILS	PLANTS	CARRIER OILS
Self-serenity	Amyris, birch, celery, clary sage, cypress, geranium, jasmine, lavender, litsea, peppermint, rose	Aloe, cilantro, coffee, coriander, gardenia, heather, hyacinth, lavender, magnolia flowers, narcissus, passion flower, peppermint, plum, rose, skullcap, tuberose, vervain, violet	Almond, apricot, borage, cranberry, rosehip
Self-expression	Amyris, birch, celery, clary sage, cypress, geranium, jasmine, litsea, peppermint, rose	Carnation, citronella, fennel, gingko, horehound, mistletoe, vervain, violet	Almond, apricot, cranberry, pomegranate, rosehip
Self-devotion	Amyris, birch, celery, clary sage, cypress, geranium, jasmine, litsea, peppermint, rose	Magnolia, narcissus, skullcap, sweet pea, thyme	Almond, camellia, evening primrose, grape, pomegranate, rosehip, sunflower

Spiritual Well-Being Bath Vinegar

Earlier this year I realized how much I needed to clear and protect my energy, so I started adding elecampane and blessed thistle tinctures to my bath a couple of times a month. Doing that helped a lot, but I wanted something a little more powerful. Vinegar also has purifying properties, and thyme is probably my second favorite herb for well-being. I added Icelandic moss at the last minute because I felt intuitively called to it without knowing why. I don't really use Icelandic moss spiritually, but upon looking it up I found it has powerful clearing properties as well.

It's so wonderful to trust your intuition, and it ends up being spot on. I've included this recipe because taking care of your energy is an act of self-devotion. Like most things in this book, it's a practice of you saying you matter.

- 1–2 thyme sprigs or 1 tsp dried thyme
- 1 tbs dried Icelandic moss
- 1 tbs dried elecampane
- 1 tsp dried blessed thistle
- ½ cup white vinegar
- 1 tsp glycerin
- 20 drops of hemlock spruce essential oil
- 2 drops of mugwort essential oil

Add the herbs to a small bottle or jar and cover them with the vinegar, glycerin and essential oils. Tightly cap the bottle and shake it gently to distribute the contents. Store in a cool, dark place for three to four days, shaking periodically.

To use, shake the bottle well, add 1 to 2 tablespoons of the liquid to warm water and swish before stepping in to disperse. Soak and enjoy. Don't strain the remaining liquid; it will get stronger over time.

Restore your spirit daily ritual

You give away your energy in small ways each and every day. Every time you come in contact with someone you are exchanging a bit of energy: they take a little piece of you, and you take a small part of them. You also give away your energy and power in your thoughts and memories. Every time you have a hypothetical argument with someone in your mind or you replay events, fixating on little details, you are investing energy. Every time you say things such as "I'm so stupid" or "I should've known better," you're using up a bit of your energy.

You can take steps to protect yourself and make it harder for others to use up your energy and you can clear the energy you've picked up from other people, but do not forget to call your energy back. Doing so will fill up holes, leaks, and gaps and cuts cords that drain your energy. When you call your energy back you refuel yourself. It's really hard to shine your light when you're feeling depleted or when you don't even have enough of your own light to use for yourself.

This ritual is very simple and you only need a minute or two each day to see big results; nothing further is required. Sit in a comfortable position. Close your eyes, and imagine you're sitting in the middle of a black space with several rows and columns forming grids in every direction, right to left and up and down, infinitely. You can't see the end of the grids but you know they go on forever.

In each box of the grids there is a memory, thought, fantasy, or experience from your life, as well as all other lives you have ever lived. You don't need to know the details: just imagine each grid playing like a movie in the background.

Place your hands palm down on your knees and begin to imagine drawing energy from each of the grid squares. Visualize the energy swirling around you and then returning to your spirit, filling in any holes, leaks, and empty spaces. The more energy you call back the more your light returns and the brighter you shine. Continue calling back your energy for no less than one minute.

When you're finished, release the streams of energy. Say a quiet "Thank you" and go on about your day.

Peacefully grounded sleep ritual

This ritual is very easy to do at night, and if you have a family then get everyone involved, about 20 minutes before bed. I think this is especially important if you have kids. For one, the soothing scents will help them sleep better but you will also be establishing healthy, beautiful habits they might take into adulthood and even pass down to their own children: a legacy of beauty, indeed. Don't skip on the light stretching of the toes and fingers, as you'd be surprised by how much stress and discomfort are carried in these areas.

You will need:

- moon milk candle (page 124) or other peaceful candle
- grounded sleep linen powder (page 129)
- tulsi chamomile moon milk (page 126)
- sweetgrass and peace hand cream (page 128)

Light the moon milk candle and sit it on a heat-tolerant surface. Dim the lights and turn off the television. Put on soothing music if you like, to help you relax.

Sprinkle a bit of the grounded sleep linen powder in your bed, focusing most of it underneath your pillow.

Whisk up the tulsi chamomile moon milk recipe, then find a peaceful spot to enjoy it such as a chair or your bed. Sit and drink the moon milk, allowing it to warm your body. When you have finished the drink, spend 5 to 10 minutes massaging the hand cream into your hands, feet, shoulders, and neck, concentrating on any areas that feel tight or sore. Massage between your fingers and toes, gently pulling each finger and each toe left, then right, to give them a nice stretch.

Bring your hands together in front of your heart, bow your head just a little, and take in one large inhale. Let out the air in one large exhale. Turn off the lights and slip into a grounded, peaceful sleep.

Goodnight!

Moon Milk Candle

Candles are much easier to make than you might believe, especially with a candle-making kit, and you can easily customize them with toppings of your choice. This is one of my favorite candle creations, which I made as an offering through my brand Spirit Element when I was still selling candles. I continue to make them for my own home till this day. As its name suggests, it was inspired by moon milks: a warming beverage that helps to destress and foster a sense of peace. The toppings are completely optional, but I think it contributes to an overall sense of beauty.

- a candle-making kit
- 1 oz | 30 ml essential oil blend
- optional toppings: powdered cinnamon, powdered ashwagandha, dried chamomile flowers, rolled oats, dried holy basil leaves

You can definitely buy all of the ingredients separately to make candles, but if you're a beginner or you don't see yourself making boxes of candles I recommend starting with a kit. It will have everything you need to make several candles at the most economical price.

Begin by weighing the wax in the kit. You can do so using the container to scoop up the wax, using two scoops for each container.

Add the wax to the pitcher included in the kit and place it on the wax melter. Alternatively, you can place the pitcher inside a pot of water and set it on the stove.

Stir with a silicone spatula to help the wax melt. Once it is completely melted, stir in 1 oz | 30 ml of essential oil for every 16 oz | 475 ml of wax, which will make two 8 oz | 250 g candles. Be sure to stir well for 2 to 3 minutes to ensure the wax and essential oils bind correctly, otherwise the fragrance may later separate from the wax.

Put the wick sticker included in the kit on the bottom of the metal foot attached to the wick. Pull the paper off the other side of the stick and do your best to place the wick in the center of the jar. Use the metal centering tool included in the kit to hold the wick steady. Repeat until you have wicked all of the candle jars.

Of course, you do not need to use the jars included in your kit; however, not all jars or containers are well suited for candles and especially not glass, which can shatter at high temperatures. If using glass, choose a thicker option or consider a metal tin.

Pour the wax into the jar and recenter the wick if necessary. Allow the candles to cool for several hours, then gently melt the top layer of wax using a hair dryer or heat gun. You only need about ⅛ in | 3 mm of melted wax on top: any more than that and your toppings will sink in and won't show on top. Sprinkle your dried toppings in your desired pattern and let the wax harden again.

Trim the wick to ¼ in | 6.5 mm. Let the candles rest for at least another 24 to 72 hours before burning, because the longer you let them cure the stronger the fragrance will be and the harder the wax will become. A harder wax means it takes less time for the candle to burn down completely, prolonging the life of the candle.

To burn, place the candle on a heat-proof surface and light it, burning for a full four hours. It's important to do this on your first burn to avoid tunneling.

Tulsi Chamomile Moon Milk

I made this moon milk to complement the moon milk candle I originally offered through my brand Spirit Element. I knew that I wanted to share it when I started making it, but I have come to really enjoy the flavor and soothing effects. I usually drink a cup of tea at night but I have lately been switching out tea with this drink, which is ultimately what inspired the peacefully grounded sleep ritual.

- 1 tsp dried chamomile or 1 chamomile teabag
- 1 tsp dried holy basil (tulsi or vana)
- 2 oz | 60 ml boiled water
- 6–8 oz | 180–240 ml oat milk or milk of your preference
- 1 tsp ashwagandha powder
- ½ tsp cinnamon powder
- few drops of vanilla extract
- honey, maple syrup or coconut sugar, to taste

Steep the chamomile and basil in the boiled water for 10 minutes to make a strong infusion, then strain the herbs from the liquid. Pour the liquid into a cup or mug and set it aside.

Warm the milk on a low heat without allowing it to come to the boil: you want it hot enough to be comforting, but not scalding. Remove the milk from the heat then whisk in the ashwagandha, cinnamon, vanilla, and sweetener.

Pour the milk mixture into the mug of tea and stir gently to combine. Enjoy!

Note: I really like the vanilla oat milk from a brand in the United States called Target, which I have found sweet enough to skip the vanilla extract and extra sweetener; however, each brand will have its own unique flavor. Play around with different milks and adjust to your taste.

Sweetgrass and Peace Hand Cream

I change my evening ritual often, but the one thing I always have is a hand cream with a nice essential oil blend. You can smell it on your hands when you sleep, especially if you are someone who sleeps with your hands near your face. The soothing scent helps the body relax and more easily slip into restful sleep, plus you'll wake up with softer hands.

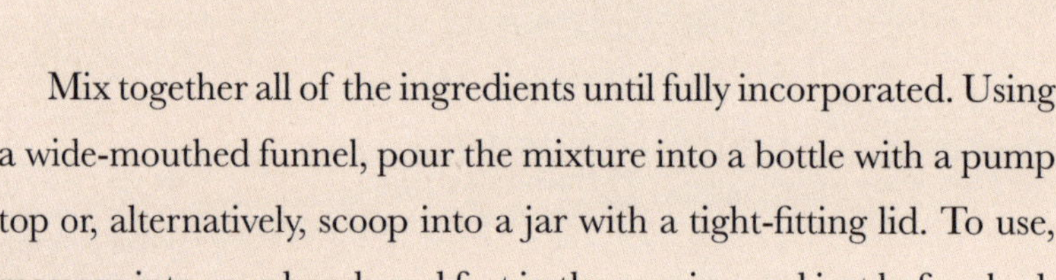

- 15 drops of angelica essential oil
- 54 drops of lavender essential oil
- 24 drops of neroli essential oil
- 9 drops of chamomile essential oil
- 54 drops of bergamot essential oil
- 1 tsp sweetgrass tincture
- 8 oz | 250 g unscented lotion or hand cream

Mix together all of the ingredients until fully incorporated. Using a wide-mouthed funnel, pour the mixture into a bottle with a pump top or, alternatively, scoop into a jar with a tight-fitting lid. To use, massage into your hands and feet in the evening and just before bed.

Magic maker tip: switch the essential oils with 80 drops of mugwort for more vivid and lucid dreaming.

Grounded Sleep Linen Powder

I have slept with many crystals over the years, but the ones I enjoy most are for grounding. Although this recipe doesn't have a crystal in it I still wanted to create a ritual that feels a little heavier and supportive. I think it's easy to overlook grounding during rest, but if you're someone who suffers from insomnia like I do then grounding energies during bedtime can really help to quiet an overactive mind. Just a tip: be conservative with how much powder you're adding to the bed, as you don't want to wake up covered in white dust!

- ¼ cup cornstarch
- ¼ cup baking soda
- 4 drops of angelica essential oil
- 7 drops of amyris essential oil
- 15 drops of lavender essential oil
- 9 drops of spruce essential oil
- 15 drops of bergamot essential oil
- 3 drops of vitamin E oil

Whisk the cornstarch and baking soda together in a small bowl, then add the essential oils and vitamin E oil. Whisk again until well blended. Store in a container with a tight-fitting lid. To use, lightly sprinkle your bed linen and the carpet with powder before going to bed.

Angel's Light Body and Anointing Oil

This oil will help restore your light so you can glow with a beauty that rivals that of the angels. Carnations have such a soft energy about them, and when used intentionally they promote beauty and creativity, while the remaining ingredients promote the intentions of radiance, peace, and grounding. You can make this oil as an anointing oil for self-devotion or as your everyday body oil. Either way, take a few moments to imagine your light glowing like that of an angel when you wear it.

- 4 oz | 120 ml apricot oil
- 2–3 food-grade carnation buds
- 25 drops of angelica essential oil
- 25 drops of lavender essential oil

Steep the apricot oil with the carnation flowers by adding the ingredients to a double boiler, small crockpot (my preferred method), or to a bowl sitting on top of a pot of simmering water. Cook on low for 1 hour, then remove from heat and cool. Strain the carnations from the oil using a coffee filter placed inside of a fine mesh strainer. Discard or compost the plant material. Add the essential oils to the infused apricot oil and mix well, then pour into a bottle of your choice.

To use, rub a few drops between the palms of your hands then inhale and exhale the scent for three to five breaths. Dab a little over your heart space and the bottoms of your feet, and massage a little into your scalp.

To use as a daily moisturizer, add 1 tablespoon of the steeped apricot oil to 4 oz | 120 ml of jojoba oil, then add the essential oils.

Self-devotion perfume

Every now and then I make a perfume I fall in love with immediately. It usually takes many variations, spread over at least a couple of weeks, to make a fragrance, but this one was a winner right from the beginning. The perfume smells like a sacred temple and no wonder, since many of the oils listed are commonly used in sacred rites and to adorn sacred places. The touch of sage gives it that smoky scent reminiscent of incense. As always, the essential oil blend can be added to a diffuser, which I have going at my desk right now as I write this.

- rose petals, if desired
- 16 drops of amyris essential oil
- 12 drops of geranium essential oil
- 6 drops of lavender essential oil
- 6 drops of sage essential oil
- vitamin E capsule
- ½ oz | 15 ml camellia seed oil

Slip the desired amount of rose petals into a small bottle, ideally a decorative one that feels luxe or special. Add the essential oils and squeeze contents of the vitamin E capsule into the bottle.

Fill the bottle with the camellia seed oil and tightly cap. Gently shake the bottle to blend the contents, then place the bottle beneath your pillow. Sleep with the bottle for one night and use it when desired to adore yourself.

State out loud: *"I vow to have deep love and respect for myself. I will worship myself as sacred and will only seek people and experiences that see the gloriousness of my authentic self."*

PART III

NURTURING OUTER BEAUTY

Before we dive into some beauty remedies for the body, I wanted to share with you a few best practices that everyone should consider incorporating into their beauty routine. In addition to that I've included a variety of updated beauty bases, which I always include in my book because you can customize them for your own needs. As well, my bases evolve over time, and I always want you to have the most updated versions of them. The bases in this chapter are the ones I'm currently loving, at least at the time of writing. To customize them, simply draw inspiration from the list of beauty allies in the book or use the ingredients you feel drawn to.

CHAPTER 6

EVERYDAY BEAUTY

BEAUTY BEST PRACTICES

Beauty is about individuality: it's about the subtle ways you're different from everyone else, and enhancing these unique qualities. There isn't a one size fits all approach to beauty, which also means your beauty practice is going to ebb and flow and evolve over time, but there are a few things you should always keep in mind when it comes to your beauty care. Below are my beauty best practices for creating a strong foundation for your uniqueness to shine. These are things everyone should keep in mind regardless of your skin, nail, or hair type, or the kind of lifestyle you have.

Hydration is key

There's a reason why the health tip about the importance of drinking plenty of water is such a cliche: because it's true! Staying hydrated is probably the best and easiest thing you can do to ensure you look and feel your best. If your body is dehydrated, then having moisturizing cream or shampoo isn't going to do much over the long term. It might help at first, but after a day or even a few hours your body will still be devoid of moisture and the conditions associated with that will persist. Aim to drink anywhere between 60 to 100 ounces | 2 to 3 liters of water a day to nourish your body from the inside out. This will create a beautiful foundation that will allow the rest of your routine to enhance an already-glowing body.

You may also wish to consider adding electrolytes to your water intake for an extra boost of hydration. Also note that while water is the best source of moisture, there are plenty of foods and especially fruits and vegetables that can aid in hydration such as cucumbers, watermelon, lettuce, celery, and tomatoes. They will contribute to good hydration and provide added vitamins and minerals.

Body mindfulness

There are so many things that can affect what your body needs to feel healthy, nourished, and beautiful. Changes in the weather, diet, what you wear, where you vacation, or whether you're feeling more stressed than usual can have a huge impact on how your nails, skin, and hair behave. For example, I've had dry skin all my life, but it got even worse when I installed a new heating and air-conditioning system in my home a few years ago. I didn't have central air and heat prior to that, so running the heater or AC all day never factored into my skincare routine. However, when I started using the system I noticed I felt dehydrated all of the time, particularly with the heater. Thus, my routine needed to change to combat my new living conditions.

Even everyday changes to small things such as the sheets you put on your bed can alter your body's needs, so staying mindful of them will arm you with information that lets you know what your immediate concerns are. Sometimes your body will need more moisture, while at other times you may need to reduce the number of products you use. Any changes to the look, feel, and texture of your body is a sign that your self-care routine also needs an update.

Switch it up

Remember when I said beauty care isn't a one size fits all kind of thing? That's also true when it comes to variety. Your body needs more than one thing at a time. Hair, for example, needs strength and moisture. If you only use products for moisture all the time then you're missing out on the other half of the equation, which ironically can lead to dryness and brittleness. Consider switching back and forth between strengthening and hydrating products to keep your hair looking luscious and full.

The same thing goes for skin. You can switch up your body and face washes, moisturizers, toners, creams and more to ensure your body gets everything it needs to thrive. Here are a few combinations to try:

- Have different products for morning versus the evening. Consider lighter, more hydrating products during the day. Your body is essentially dehydrated when you wake up, so having products with high moisture content can help to revive parched skin and hair. Richer emollient products are better for night time, when your body goes into rest and repair mode.
- Try mixing your routine up for the weekends, especially if you leave your home for work. Your home's environment is going to be completely different from your work one, thus your routine should match the difference.
- For those of you with a menstrual cycle, consider altering your routine based on each phase. Hormone changes can make a big difference in your body's needs. You may need products that tackle oiliness to prevent clogged pores and breakouts just before your period is

starting, or to focus on nourishing products rather than harsh exfoliants or chemicals during your menstrual phase. I highly recommend downloading an app that will help you understand each menstrual phase, and also keeping a journal of how your body behaves during your cycle, so you can adjust accordingly. Likewise, hormonal shifts can occur during and after pregnancy that may also require a different approach to your beauty routine.

- Changes in activity level is a big one. If you're a really active person you may want to consider using a different set of products after intense activity. For me, it is absolutely essential to use a wash with salicylic acid on my back and face to avoid breakouts after the gym. However, I would never use salicylic acid every day because it would totally dry out my skin, so I have a completely different set of products to use on days when I'm not very active.

Please do note that when making changes to your self-care routine it's important to take a conservative approach. Change one thing at a time, and wait at least a week before making any adjustments. If you change up your whole routine at once you'll have no way of knowing what's working and what isn't working, but if you change just one thing within one to two weeks you should be able to see how your body responds to it and can make an informed decision from there. I am always on the hunt for new self-care whether I make it myself or purchase it.

I recently wanted to try out a face serum so I bought one. I started using it, and within two days I noticed my skin breaking out so I stopped using it. Within the week my skin cleared up, and it became obvious that the serum didn't agree with my body. If I had changed my facial cleanser and moisturizer and added the serum all at the same time I wouldn't have known which of the three led to the breakout. By focusing on one product at a time I was able to pinpoint the exact reason why I experienced trouble, and I knew exactly what to do to fix it.

Soak it in

I'm a huge fan of layering products, especially on the face and body. I mix lotions and creams all the time, but it's important to do it in a way that doesn't lead to clogged pores. This is particularly so on your face. I'm not one for the 20-step beauty routine, but remember that it doesn't matter what I think if it makes you feel beautiful. If that's your jam, then you do you.

Whether you're layering two products or 12 it's important to let each layer soak in before moving on to the next, because each product has a function that needs time to work its magic. Generally, you want to wait until your skin no longer feels slick before moving on to the next layer. Failing to do so could leave you with products that mix and create interesting textures that could feel similar to peeling skin, or clumps of products that dry on top of your skin.

This also applies to the rest of your body, although when it comes to your hair you should massage through your leave-in conditioner before drying your hair. Doing so while your hair is still wet and warm means the cuticles are open and the conditioner will actually soak in rather than sitting on top, which is often the case when hair becomes cold and the cuticles close.

Wear sunscreen

Sunscreen is an everyday job: it doesn't matter whether it's sunny or raining, you should be wearing sunscreen over your entire body. Sun rays don't disappear just because it's cloudy. In fact, they can penetrate through clouds, and if you aren't wearing sunscreen that also means they are penetrating your skin. If nothing else, wearing sunscreen daily regardless of the weather creates a habit, so when it is sunny you won't forget. You should also reapply sunscreen throughout the day, as it tends to wear off. Don't forget to also put sunscreen on your lips and the backs of your hands. The skin on these areas is very thin and thus prone to more damage and signs of ageing.

Hands and ageing

I'll never forget the first time I heard that your hands show signs of ageing before your face does, and I've been obsessed with hand care ever since. Even though we hear this, hands are still often neglected. I put whatever goes on my face on the backs of my hands and that includes toner, any serum I'm using, moisturizer, and sunscreen. My hands have never looked better. It's also ideal to keep bottles of lotion or hand cream nearby to reapply throughout the day, especially if you wash your hands a lot or use a lot of hand sanitizer.

Take things slowly

Finally, slow down, darling. Your body is precious and needs to be treated that way. I get it: we're all busy and sometimes it's a struggle to slap some lotion on, let alone massage it gingerly into your skin. However, treating your body with care will pay you back tenfold. Soft, gentle movements over time will help reduce wrinkles and fine lines, loss of elasticity and, most importantly, contribute to an overall feeling of self-love and respect.

CRAFTING A BEAUTY ALTAR

Having a dedicated beauty altar or vanity is such a beautiful way to devote yourself to having more beauty in your life. This space will serve as your private area that's all about looking and feeling your best. Of course, you'll want to have things that contribute to self-care, such as your skincare, perfumes, perhaps makeup, hair products, and styling tools, but there are other enhancements you may wish to have. Additionally, this is a beautiful space so keep it clean and clutter free, only allowing your most cherished items to remain there. Some other things to consider are:

- candles and incense burner or aromatherapy diffuser
- a vase with fresh flowers, changed weekly, or faux flowers
- decorative jewelry boxes or cases
- photos of your beauty icons
- a beautiful hand mirror
- good lighting
- decorative pots and bottles you can pour your products into
- a beautiful glass or teacup and saucer to drink from while you get ready
- a luxurious chair to sit in

You may also wish to enhance the overall experience by wearing a plush robe and soft slippers.

Sacred adornment dedication ritual

Anything can be sacred with the right intention, even jewelry. You can dedicate jewelry to a specific purpose the same way you might dedicate a ritual tool such as a journal. Reserve this ritual for your most sacred jewelry, those items that are heirlooms or heirlooms in the making, or items that make you feel as though you are on top of the world when you wear them. It doesn't matter how much the jewelry costs, as long as it gives you a sense of empowerment and beauty.

- 4 white or pink candles
- a beautiful dish
- flowers, crystals, trinkets, statues, and other symbols of beauty
- dried hawthorn leaf for promoting happiness and success
- dried rose petals for happiness and self-love
- dried jasmine flowers for beauty and confidence
- rose quartz crystal/s for universal love and self-healing
- jewelry that makes you feel powerful or beautiful

Place the candles on a working altar or table in a square formation. Place the dish in the center, then surround the candles and dish with the flowers, crystals, trinkets, statues, and any other symbols of beauty and self-confidence you'd like to include. Don't worry about the traditional meanings of these items: they should be personal to you and represent what you believe to be beautiful.

Light the candles. Add a pinch or two of each of the plant materials and at least one piece of rose quartz to a beautiful dish or bowl. You'll want something that is pretty to look at and brings you joy when you see it.

Hold each piece of jewelry in your hands, one at a time. You may wish to bring the jewelry to your heart or solar plexus space. Take a deep breath, then say this affirmation:

I dedicate this jewelry to the purpose of invoking personal power.
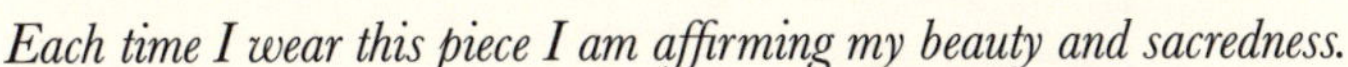
Each time I wear this piece I am affirming my beauty and sacredness.
Each time I wear this piece I am acknowledging my unlimited worth.
Each time I wear this piece I am reminded of my magnificence.
So it is.

Gently place the jewelry in the dish and repeat with the remaining pieces of jewelry. Take a moment or two to thank your jewelry for holding your intentions. Extinguish the candles and place your dish where you can see it every morning, such as on your beauty altar (see page 144).

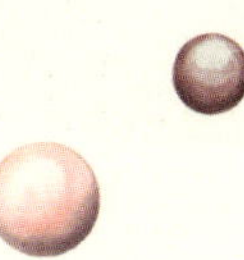

HANDMADE SAFETY

Before charging into making your own beauty potions it's important to make sure you're making safe and ethical products. Natural skincare has a very short lifespan, and many of the things you make in this book will only last a few days in the refrigerator. Pretty much anything containing water will need to be tossed out after a week at the latest. However, there are some things that can withstand a longer shelf life. Typically, oil- or alcohol-based products such as infused oils or bathing cordials can last several months and up to several years after making them, but if anything develops a strange smell or film then it's time to toss it away.

The way to avoid having to toss out too much is to make smaller batches, which actually works to your favor. As I mentioned earlier in this chapter, your body's needs are going to change. You might need a heavier oil this time of year versus a few months ago, or more water-based products now versus last week. Making smaller batches will allow you to make and use what you need without being wasteful, while also giving you more freedom to customize your beauty potions based on your body's immediate needs.

BEAUTY BASES

Having beauty bases on hand will make your beauty journey so much easier and more convenient. You can buy bases, of course, and I do so all of the time, but it's also nice to customize as much of your beauty potions as possible. Making your own bases will allow you to do just that. In this section you'll find a selection of base recipes you can customize to fit your needs. You can also make up large batches of each recipe to keep on hand in a beauty cabinet, so that when you want to focus on your beauty care you won't have to go through too much trouble to whip something together.

As your body's needs change, sometimes as little as one hour to the next, being able to customize a recipe on a dime without having to throw out a large batch of something you've made because it didn't work for your body's needs or because it worked yesterday and not today is a much more mindful way to approach custom beauty care.

Basic alcohol tincture

How I make tinctures is pretty straightforward. There is a more measured way to do it, but I've included the simple, folk method I believe is perfectly fine for home use. I will say that for a long time I mostly used vodka, but I have recently switched to the grain alcohol Everclear. It's more expensive, but the higher proof means you don't have to worry too much about excess water getting into your tincture. Everclear is a must if you're using fresh ingredients, as I have done more recently.

- 8 oz | 250 ml jar with a tight-fighting lid
- plant material of your choice
- high-proof alcohol
- wax paper
- cheesecloth or coffee filters
- amber-colored dropper bottle

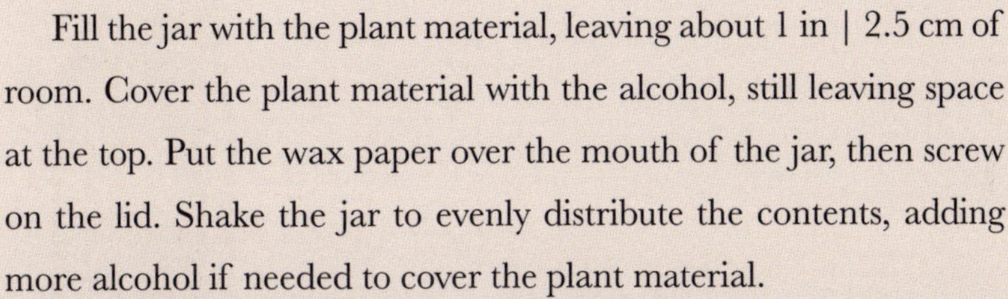

Fill the jar with the plant material, leaving about 1 in | 2.5 cm of room. Cover the plant material with the alcohol, still leaving space at the top. Put the wax paper over the mouth of the jar, then screw on the lid. Shake the jar to evenly distribute the contents, adding more alcohol if needed to cover the plant material.

Label the jar with the name and date, then place it in a dark cabinet or space. Shake the jar every day for two to four weeks: the longer it sits the more potent it will be.

Strain the plant material through the cheesecloth or coffee filter, pressing out as much of the oil as possible. Compost the plant material. Pour the tincture into the dropper bottle and label. Add ½ to 1 teaspoon of tincture to water-based formulas as desired.

Basic oil infusion

A basic oil infusion is one of the best ways to customize creams, balms, and any other apothecary recipe requiring a vegetable oil. It's also one of the most nourishing ways to incorporate plant material into your beauty care, and allows you to mix and match ingredients with ease. a simple infused oil can be used as is for a natural body and hair oil or a healing skin treat, or added to your bath. You can also use them in more complicated recipes such as conditioners and salves.

- dried herbs
- carrier oil or blend of oils
- cheesecloth
- a jar with tight-fitting lid

Maceration method: add the desired herbs to a jar, filling to three-quarters of the way full. Pour in enough oil to completely fill the jar. Cover the jar with a piece of cheesecloth and cap it with the lid. Keep the jar in a sunny or warm space for two to four weeks, shaking the mixture daily and especially if using cheesecloth.

Strain the mixture through the cheesecloth and compost the plant material. Store the mixture in a jar or bottle with a tight lid for up to one year. Throw away immediately if the oil smells rancid or develops any sign of bacterial growth.

Crockpot method: add the desired herbs to a small crockpot or double broiler and pour over enough oil to completely cover the plants. Cook over a low for two to three hours, then remove from the heat and allow to cool. Strain the mixture and store it following the directions for the maceration method.

Bath and Body Oil Base Recipe

Any infused oil is essentially an oil-based tincture. You can use just about any combination of vegetable oils. I tend to limit the more precious ones such as borage to small amounts, though if you're happy to use an entire cup of borage oil then feel free to do so. You can also skip the plant-infused body oil if you like, but infusing plants into oils will allow you to add an extra layer of beauty and magic.

- 30 drops of essential oil
- 8 oz | 250 ml glass bottle with a lid
- 1 cup plant-infused body oil
- ½ tbs precious oil such as rosehip, borage, or pomegranate

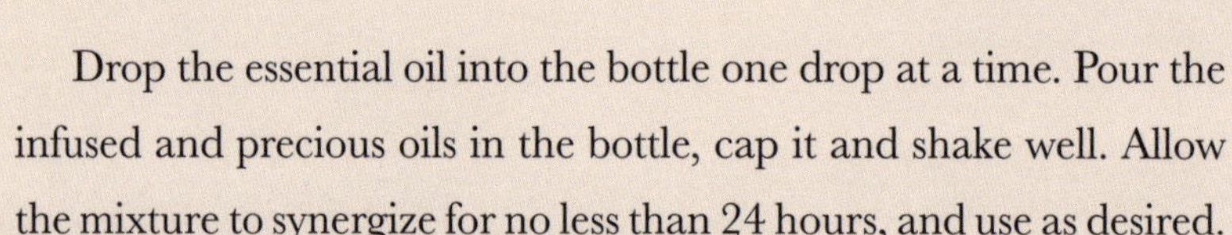

Drop the essential oil into the bottle one drop at a time. Pour the infused and precious oils in the bottle, cap it and shake well. Allow the mixture to synergize for no less than 24 hours, and use as desired.

BASIC SALVE RECIPE

This is my basic, go-to salve recipe that I customize based on my needs, and is a must have in any apothecary cabinet. I use these salve variations for everything from dry skin to healing wounds and scars. I also use salves for inner beauty such as the spirit ointment to uplight energy (page 91). You can customize the carrier oil by infusing it with a variety of plant materials; see page 152.

- 1 oz | 30 g beeswax
- 4 oz | 120 ml infused carrier oil or a mixture of oils
- 1 tbs shea butter
- 20 drops of essential oil

Add all of the ingredients to a double boiler, stirring regularly to prevent burning. Once melted, remove from the heat and allow the mixture to cool slightly, then add the desired essential oils.

Pour or ladle the mixture into a heat-proof container or tin while the mixture is still liquid. Allow the mixture to cool and harden, then cap it with a tight-fitting lid. Store in a cool, dark place for up to one year. Basic salves can be kept in the refrigerator on hot days to prevent them from melting. To use, scoop a bit up with your fingers, gently warm the mixture between your palms and apply as needed.

Body Cream Base Recipe

This is the easiest cream base you will ever have, as it doesn't require any special equipment or knowledge about how to properly emulsify oils and waters. Buying a lotion base also means it has preservatives, so you won't have to worry about it spoiling. Generally, you can add oils, waters, fragrances, and tinctures without needing to worry about bacteria growth or having to store the cream in the refrigerator.

- 16 oz | 455 g unscented lotion or cream
- 1 tsp essential oil or essential oil blend
- squeeze bottle or one with a pump top

Blend the lotion and essential oil together in a medium-sized bowl. Using a funnel, gently spoon the lotion into the bottle, allowing it time to settle before adding another spoonful. Use as desired within one year.

Spray base recipe

Sprays are so fun and easy to customize. Try mixing up your water content with other water-based ingredients such as wine, tinctures, extracts, or teas. You can also make a spray using solely alcohol, which will help the spray last longer. Sprays made with teas will need to be refrigerated and can be kept for up to five days.

- 1 tsp vodka or high-proof alcohol, optional
- 50 drops of essential oil
- 8 oz | 250 ml bottle with a spray top
- 6 oz | 180 ml distilled water
- 2 oz | 60 ml hydrosol

Mix the alcohol with the essential oil and add to the bottle, or put the essential oil directly in the bottle if you're not using the alcohol. Top off with the water and hydrosol and tightly screw on the spray top. Allow the mixture to synergize for no less than 24 hours.

Shake well before each use, and use as desired to lightly scent a room and invoke the energy of this spray.

Body Scrub Base Recipe

I always have a body scrub at the ready. If you have dry skin like me, then a body scrub is going to be your best friend. It's also really great for setting a foundation for shaving. Scrub the skin you want to shave the night before, and you will have the closest shave ever the next day. It's best to shave in the morning if you can as your skin and muscles swell as you move throughout the day, meaning you won't be able to shave as much of the hair follicle as possible later in the day.

- 1 cup fine salt or sugar
- 1–2 tsp powdered herbs and/or spices
- ¼ cup oil
- 30 drops of essential oil

Whisk together the salt or sugar in a bowl with the herbs and spices. Using a spoon, combine the dry mixture with the oil. Stir well to blend the ingredients, then add the essential oil. Spoon into a container with a tight lid.

To apply, massage a small amount onto moist skin, rubbing in a counterclockwise motion, then rinse. Use within six to eight months. Refrigeration is not required.

SHAMPOO BASE RECIPE

As you can no doubt imagine I've made a lot of different shampoos over the years, and this is probably the thing I'm always tweaking the most. So much of my current career is the result of a decision I made years ago, which was to take my hair health seriously. This is my current go-to, home-made shampoo recipe.

- 1 oz | 30 ml glycerin
- 1 tbs carrier oil (you can also use an infused oil)
- 4 oz | 120 g unscented shampoo or Castile soap
- 2 tsp plant extract or tincture
- ½ tsp essential oil or essential oil blend

Blend together the glycerin and carrier oil in a small bowl until combined. Add the shampoo and half of the extract or tincture, then blend again until smooth. Gently mix the essential oil or oil blend into the shampoo mixture.

Wash your hair with the shampoo, rinse it then follow with a conditioner. You can also turn this recipe into an easy base conditioner recipe by replacing the shampoo with an unscented conditioner.

Beauty tip: I recommend you add 1 tablespoon of aloe vera gel for extra nourishment, mixing it in along with the glycerin and carrier oil.

Body Wash Base Recipe

I used to use Castile soap for body washes, and while you still can if you choose I prefer to use unscented soap now as it offers more of a lather. I love the feeling of soft, rich bubbles against my skin, which feels a bit more luxurious than the low-suds option.

- ½ cup distilled water
- 3–4 tbs herb material of your choice
- 8 oz | 250 g Castile soap or unscented liquid soap
- ½ cup hydrosol
- 20 drops of essential oil
- 1 tsp carrier oil

Bring the distilled water to the boil in a small saucepan, then turn off the heat. Add the herb material, cover it and allow the mixture to steep and cool for at least 30 to 45 minutes. Strain and compost the herbs.

Add the Castile soap, hydrosol, essential oil and carrier oil to the herbal base and mix well. Pour into a bottle with a tight-fitting lid. This mixture can be kept in the refrigerator for three to four weeks.

CHAPTER 7

BEAUTIFUL HAIR

Many moons ago, before I started Spirit Element, I had another apothecary called 18 & Sweet Rose, named after my grandmother. I share a birthday with her: November 18. My grandmother was known by the name "Sweet," and she was famous for her rose garden. She's also the reason why I'm such a great gardener, and much of my garden went into the beauty products I created under this label – which had nothing to do with spirituality. This brand was all about being beautiful, but my life took me in a different direction.

However, I have so many recipes that were so luscious and nourishing that to this day people still ask me to make special batches for them to purchase. These recipes are so precious to me, which is why I'm choosing to share them here with you. Most of the recipes in this chapter are from my 18 & Sweet Rose days, and all of them are in the pursuit of looking and feeling your best.

ULTRA NOURISHING HAIR OIL

This hair oil is very rich and protective. If you tend to have dry or fragile hair, then this is for you. It really amplifies any shampoo or conditioner you add it to, or you can massage a few drops on wet hair to lock in moisture. For a very nourishing treat, massage it into your scalp and down the strands of hair the night before washing.

- 1 tsp fenugreek
- 1 tsp mullein
- 1 tsp dandelion root
- 2 tsp catnip
- 2 tsp marshmallow root
- 2 tsp dried rosemary
- ½ aloe vera leaf, chopped
- 3 tsp nettle leaf
- olive oil
- avocado oil

- argan oil
- 1 tsp rosemary essential oil
- cheesecloth

Add the plants to a small crockpot or double broiler and pour over enough of the oils to completely cover them. Cook on low for two to three hours, then remove from the heat and allow to cool.

Strain the mixture through cheesecloth and compost the plant material. Pour the mixture and essential oil into a jar or bottle with a tight-fitting lid and keep for up to one year. Throw away immediately if the oil smells rancid or develops any sign of bacterial growth.

To use, gently warm a small amount of the oil between your palms then apply to your hair from the roots to the ends. Using your fingertips, massage a bit more into your scalp as well, working in circular motions to stimulate the hair follicles. Use daily or as needed.

Beauty tip: keep some of the mixture in a dropper bottle. Add a few drops to brush bristles before brushing your hair for better distribution.

Fig- and Thyme-Infused Hair Oil

Before I got into the spiritual properties of plants I was obsessed with their benefits for beauty. I learned that figs are great for hair, as they help to reduce breakage and hair loss while also acting as an effective conditioner. The combination of figs, catnip, and marshmallow root is a rockstar combination that I frequently use. This infused oil is great to work into your scalp and down through the hair strands the night before washing and periodically throughout the week, for hair oiling or to add extra hair production. Of course, you can also add it to other haircare products such as shampoos and conditioners for extra nourishment.

- 2 tbs dried figs, chopped
- 2 tbs dried catnip
- 1 tbs dried marshmallow root
- ½ cup olive oil
- ½ cup avocado oil
- 2 tbs castor oil
- cheesecloth
- 20 drops of thyme essential oil

Add the figs, catnip, and marshmallow root to a small crockpot or double broiler. Pour the olive, avocado and castor oils on top to completely cover the plants. Cook on low for two to three hours, then remove from heat and allow to cool.

Strain the mixture through the cheesecloth and compost the plant material. Pour the mixture and essential oil into a jar or bottle with a tight-fitting lid and keep for up to one year. Throw away immediately if the oil smells rancid or develops any sign of bacterial growth.

Fig and Thyme Nourishing Shampoo

While you're making the fig- and thyme-infused hair oil (page 166) I highly recommend making this shampoo as well, which uses pretty much the same ingredients. Catnip and marshmallow root have been my go-to hair ingredients for probably 12 years now, and they never let me down. They always leave my hair feeling soft and easy to manage, while fig is especially great for promoting hair growth.

- 2 cups distilled water
- 2 tbs dried figs, chopped
- 1 tbs dried catnip
- 1 tbs dried marshmallow root
- 1 tsp dried thyme
- 3 oz | 90 g Castile soap
- 1 tsp fig-infused oil
- 20 drops of lavender essential oil
- 10 drops of orange essential oil
- 10 drops of palma rosa essential oil
- 5 drops of thyme essential oil
- 1 tbs aloe vera gel

Bring the distilled water to a simmer in a small saucepan. Add the figs and herbs to a heat-safe cup and pour the boiled water over the herbs. Cover with a tea towel and steep for one hour.

Strain and compost the herbs. Pour the tea mixture into a pourable bottle or one with a pump top. Add the Castile soap, fig-infused oil, essential oils, and aloe vera gel. Cap tightly, then gently shake the contents well before each use.

This shampoo creates a low-suds formula. To use, dampen your hair, pump or squeeze about one-quarter cup of the shampoo directly onto your scalp and massage in using wet hands. Work down through the hair strains, adding more shampoo if it's needed for longer hair. Rinse well and follow with the apple harvest hair conditioner (page 170).

Apple Harvest Hair Conditioner

Apples are nearly 90 percent water, so it's no wonder they are wonderfully hydrating to the skin and hair. Many moons ago I began working with apples in haircare, and I was blown away by how nourishing they are for the scalp and hair strands. Licorice root and catnip share similar hydrating properties, and this blend of ingredients is perfect for the cold months when hair needs some extra love.

- 1 apple, diced
- 1 tbs dried catnip
- 1 tsp dandelion root
- 1 tsp dried licorice root
- 2 oz | 60 ml water
- 1 tsp vegetable glycerin or honey
- 1 cup unscented conditioner
- 20 drops of rosemary essential oil

To make a hair tea, combine the apple, catnip, dandelion root, licorice root, and water in a saucepan and bring to a boil. Cover and remove from the heat, then allow the mixture to steep until cool. Strain the liquid and compost the plant material.

Combine the apple tea mixture with the vegetable glycerin or honey. Slowly mix the unscented conditioner into the apple mixture, stirring until combined. Mix in the rosemary essential oil until well combined.

To use, comb the conditioner through freshly washed hair and leave on for no more than 20 minutes. Rinse, then style your hair as usual.

Beauty tip: add a small amount of water to activate surfactants in the conditioner for better slip while using less product.

Intensive Hair Mask

This is my go-to mask when my hair needs to be revived. Sometimes life gets busy and my hair is usually the first thing I ignore when that's the case, and because I have a head full of curls any neglect results in needing a lot of extra care to bring my hair back to life. This conditioner will restore manageability, shine, and strength. If you don't already have one I highly recommend getting a hair steamer, which opens the hair follicle and allows the conditioner to fully penetrate and nourish your hair.

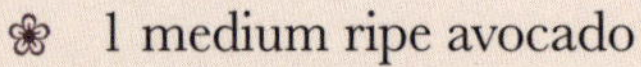

- 1 medium ripe avocado
- 2 tbs aloe vera gel
- 2 tbs fig- and thyme-infused hair oil (page 166)
- ¼ cup vegetable glycerin
- 1 cup unscented conditioner
- 15 drops of cedarwood essential oil
- 3 drops of tea tree oil

Blend together the avocado, aloe vera gel, ultra-nourishing infused hair oil, and glycerin in a small food processor until blended. Add the conditioner and essential oils and blend again until smooth.

Massage the mixture into clean, damp hair and comb through with a wide-toothed comb. Cover with a shower cap and leave for 30 minutes, or use a hair steamer for ultra-deep penetration. Rinse well and follow up with a hair rinse or leave-in conditioner.

Catnip Hair Rinse

I've shared this recipe before, but I think it's worth sharing again. Catnip is one of my favorite beauty herbs for hair. The leaves are pillowy soft and, like the leaves, catnip leaves your hair soft to the touch and much more manageable. In fact, many women and men swear by this herb to reduce split ends and condition hair. With continued use catnip is reported to eliminate split ends altogether and is often referred to as a conditioner alternative.

Catnip or catmint is part of the mint family and carries similar astringent properties as its cousin, peppermint. Not only will this recipe leave your hair feeling much softer, but you will also find a decrease in dandruff and overall scalp irritation.

Many people use a catnip rinse without conditioner with much success. However, I am very attached to conditioner: it was the first beauty product I ever made. I personally believe you can never have too much conditioner or too many different kinds, and I continue to use both conditioner and this catnip rinse. The rinse can be used before or after conditioner, depending on your hair type. For dry or damaged hair use the rinse before applying conditioner, and with oily and fine hair use the rinse after conditioner.

- 2 cups boiling water
- 1–2 tbs catnip
- 1 tsp red clover herb
- 1 tsp chamomile
- 1 tsp fenugreek, optional
- 1 tsp olive or castor oil
- 5 drops of rosemary essential oil
- 5 drops of sage essential oil
- 1 tbs apple cider vinegar or lemon juice (omit if you aren't rinsing it out)

Pour the boiling water over the herbs and allow to steep until the mixture has reached room temperature. Add the oils and vinegar and mix well. Dip the ends of your hair into the mixture, then pour the remaining liquid over your scalp and massage, working the liquid through the strands of hair. Cover your hair with a plastic cap or warm towel and sit for 15 minutes, then rinse your hair and style it as usual.

CHAPTER 8

A BEAUTIFUL BODY

The recipes in this chapter are dedicated to soft skin and luxurious self-care. For years I thought I was allergic to wool and cashmere, only to discover I just had dry skin and wasn't tending to my beautiful body properly. I started making it a point to incorporate much of what you find here in my weekly self-care practice, and I soon came to realize I wasn't allergic at all: my skin was just irritated and needed some love. I can't say for certain you will have the same experience if wool irritates your skin, but I can say these recipes will contribute to nourishing and calming skin.

As a reminder: inner hydration is key. I incorporated these recipes into my self-routine, but I also make it a point to drink a lot more water these days.

Calming Body Scrub

Regular exfoliation is key for soft skin. Your body is always shedding skin cells, but it could use a little help from time to time. a weekly or bi-weekly scrub will gently loosen skin cells to reveal new, fresh, glowing skin underneath. What I love about this recipe is that the ingredients are naturally soothing to skin, reducing the irritation that scrubs can sometimes cause. You can use regular sugar for this recipe but I prefer the finer castor sugar, which isn't as harsh. If you can't find castor sugar, pulse one cup of regular sugar in a food processor for 30 seconds to reduce the size of the grains.

- 1 cup castor sugar
- 1 tsp orange peel granules
- ½ tsp marjoram powder
- ½ tsp rose powder
- ¼ cup rosehip oil
- 1 tbs melted shea butter

- ½ tsp vanilla extract
- 20 drops of marjoram essential oil
- 5 drops of sandalwood essential oil

Whisk together the castor sugar, orange peel granules, marjoram powder, and rose powder in a bowl. In a separate bowl or cup mix together the rosehip oil, shea butter, vanilla extract, and essential oils. Stir together the two mixtures with a spoon until well combined.

Spoon the mixture into a container with a tight-fitting lid. To apply, gently massage a small amount onto moist skin, rubbing in a counterclockwise motion, then rinse. Use within six to eight months; refrigeration is not required.

Soft as Roses Body Wash

Rose really is a rock star when it comes to beauty, whether you take it internally or externally. For your skin it pretty much does it all, reducing inflammation and irritation and its high vitamin C content contributing to a more even skin tone. It is also antibacterial and can help reduce dryness. Not only that: rose is very much associated with love and beauty and is said to increase confidence and attractiveness.

- 1 cup distilled water
- 2 tbs dried rosehip root
- 2 tbs dried rose petals
- 1 tbs dried lavender flowers
- 8 oz | 250 g Castile soap (preferably rose, but lavender is also nice)
- 2 tsp honey or vegetable glycerin
- 10 drops of rose absolute
- 5 drops of ylang ylang essential oil
- ½ tsp sweet almond oil

Bring the water to the boil in a small saucepan, then turn off heat. Add the rosehip root, rose petals, and lavender flowers, cover and allow the mixture to steep and cool for at least 30 to 45 minutes. Strain and compost the herbs.

Add the Castile soap, honey or vegetable glycerin, essential oils, and sweet almond oil to the herbal base and mix well. Pour into a bottle with a tight-fitting lid. This mixture can be kept in the refrigerator for around one week.

Spirit of Beauty Body Lotion

This simple skin-soothing potion infused with herbal goodness is known for promoting qualities of inner beauty. Pomegranate helps you find your inner beauty, jasmine encourages confidence and worth, while mandarin encourages you to find self-compassion on days when you're being too hard on yourself. Use this blend in the morning to set the tone for the day.

- 8 oz | 250 ml unscented lotion
- ½ cup pomegranate seed oil
- ½ tsp jasmine essential oil
- 10 drops of mandarin essential oil
- dried rose petals

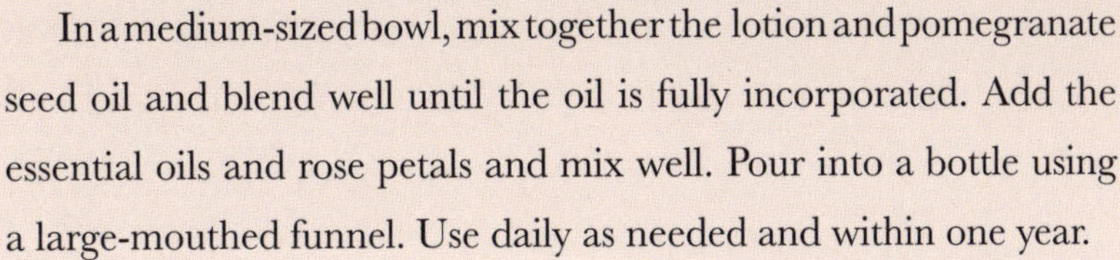

In a medium-sized bowl, mix together the lotion and pomegranate seed oil and blend well until the oil is fully incorporated. Add the essential oils and rose petals and mix well. Pour into a bottle using a large-mouthed funnel. Use daily as needed and within one year.

Invigorating Body Butter

This butter is super nourishing, as it was originally made for the winter season. Some body butters are made completely with oils and fats, so because they don't have any water they aren't really hydrating. This cream is still nice and thick but has enough water to penetrate your skin, leaving it feeling nourished and moisturized. If you can't find camellia seed oil, instead add some green tea leaves to the infused oil mixture.

- 4 oz | 120 ml peppermint hydrosol
- 1 tsp vegetable glycerin
- 2 oz | 60 g burdock, lavender and marshmallow root infused in camellia seed oil
- 2 tsp stearic acid
- 3 tsp emulsifying wax
- 1 tsp vitamin E oil
- 40 drops of lavender essential oil
- 20 drops of clove essential oil
- 20 drops of cypress essential oil

Pour the hydrosol into a glass measuring cup and place inside a saucepan containing several inches of water. Simmer until the temperature measures 160°F | 70°C. Remove from heat and mix in the glycerin.

Mix the infused oil with the stearic acid and wax in a separate glass measuring cup and place inside a saucepan containing several inches of water. Simmer until the temperature reaches 160°F | 70°C, then remove from heat. Both mixtures should stay within 3 to 4 degrees of each other once removed from the heat.

Pour the oil into a heat-proof bowl and begin mixing with a hand mixer. Slowly add the water mixture and continue to mix until the mixture cools to 120°F | 50°C. Add the vitamin E and essential oils and mix well.

Transfer the cream to a clean glass jar and store in the refrigerator for up to 15 days.

Relaxing Bathing Cordial

Baths cordials are one of my favorite things to make. They are infinitely customizable and last for years thanks to the alcohol, so you can make tons of these and keep them on hand. Alcohol is a non-abrasive exfoliant that will leave your skin feeling refreshed and soft. You can use just about any alcohol, including wine: each one will impart a different scent experience, so test them out and see what you like best. My personal favorite is brandy, which offers a rich aroma that pairs well with florals and spices. I recently found one in the back of a cabinet that had been there for years, and it smelt incredible! The longer you let it sit the richer the fragrance will be.

- ½ tbs dried lavender flowers
- ½ tbs dried marjoram
- ½ tbs dried chamomile
- ½ tbs dried rose petals
- ½ tbs dried catnip
- a large jar
- ¾ cup brandy
- ¼ cup apple cider vinegar
- 2 tsp vanilla extract
- 3 tsp vegetable oil such as olive, almond, or grapeseed
- 20 drops of marjoram essential oil

- 20 drops of grapefruit essential oil
- 15 drops of patchouli essential oil

Combine all of the dry ingredients in the jar, then top with the brandy, apple cider vinegar, and vanilla extract, being sure to cover the herbs completely. Add the oils and shake well.

Place the jar in a cool, dark place for at least three days or longer to synergize, giving it a good shake every morning. The longer you let it sit the more intense the scent will be.

To use, draw a warm bath then add 2 to 3 tablespoons to the water. Agitate the water to disperse the cordial before stepping in. Enjoy!

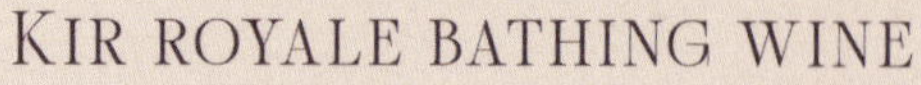

Kir Royale Bathing Wine

This one is just for fun and is a luxurious bathing treat. I was inspired by two things: *Emily in Paris,* and a character named Gin from a book series called The Bourbon Kings. This is super luxe and indulgent, which is the point. Sometimes beauty isn't about serving a function; it's just for the sake of going out of your way to make the experience gorgeous.

- 1 cinnamon stick
- 1 tsp dried rosemary
- 1 tsp dried clove
- 1 cup sparkling wine
- 1 tbs crème de cassis (blackcurrant liqueur)
- 1 tbs gin
- 20 drops of lemon essential oil

Combine all of the dry ingredients in a jar, then top with the sparkling wine, crème de cassis, gin, and lemon essential oil, completely covering the herbs. Let the mixture stand for 20 minutes to allow the sparkling wine bubbles to disperse, then put on the lid.

Place the jar in a cool, dark place for at least three days or longer to synergize, giving it a gentle shake every morning. The longer you let it sit the more intense the scent will be.

To use, draw a warm bath then add 2 to 3 tablespoons of the bathing wine to it. Agitate the water to disperse before stepping in.

Nectar Body Oil

Nectar is a really soft, really beautiful oil to use every day. It's refreshing and floral, and has just a touch of creaminess from the vetiver and vanilla. The vanilla oil is definitely a bit of a splurge, but a bottle of it will last for a very long time. As an alternative you can steep vanilla beans in the jojoba oil following the basic oil infusion recipe on (page 152), although the scent won't be nearly as strong.

- 36 drops of rose essential oil
- 20 drops of geranium essential oil
- 6 drops of vetiver essential oil
- 1 drop of spearmint essential oil
- 1 vitamin E capsule
- 36 drops of vanilla absolute oil
- 4 oz | 120 ml jojoba oil

Combine the essential oils and pour them into a small bottle. Prick the vitamin E capsule with a needle and squeeze the contents into the bottle. Top the bottle off with the vanilla and jojoba oils.

Cap the bottle and shake it well. Place the bottle on your altar to synergize for at least 24 hours, then use as you would a traditional bath and body oil or to adorn ritual tools and candles.

CHAPTER 9

BEAUTIFUL FRAGRANCES

By now you know that beauty isn't something you experience only with your eyes. Fragrance can make you just as attractive as how you look or behave, and for me personally fragrance is probably 80 percent of my self-care routine. There's nothing like taking in a scent and letting it settle you, so I've made sure to provide plenty of perfumes for body and home.

Smoked vanilla and pine perfume

This recipe is a bit involved but it's totally worth it. The added step of smoking the plant material adds a moody, mysterious and earthy quality to the perfume that you just can't replicate any other way. It's really important to use chemical-free charcoal to avoid nasty chemicals in your perfume. As for the wood shavings, experiment with different kinds of wood as each will contribute a slightly different scent to the final product.

- 1 bunch of pine needles, tied together
- 1 bunch of lavender flowers, tied together
- chemical-free charcoal briquettes
- wood shavings
- 2–3 vanilla beans, split lengthwise
- vodka or perfumer's alcohol

Allow the herbs to dry out overnight if you're using fresh pine or lavender. Keep in mind that dried lavender will work perfectly fine for this recipe as long as the buds are still on the stems, although I recommend fresh pine needles when possible.

Place the charcoal briquettes on a barbecue grill and carefully light. Once they are fully lit and have turned to embers, add the wood shavings on top and allow them to smoke. Meanwhile, add the vanilla beans, pine needles and lavender steams to a metal colander or mesh basket and place it inside the barbecue but not directly over the fire. You want about 12 in | 30 cm of space between the fire and the colander. Put the lid on top and allow the herbs to smoke for 20 to 40 minutes, rotating occasionally.

Remove the herbs from the smoke and allow them to cure overnight on a clean cloth. Add the herbs to a jar and completely cover with the vodka or perfumer's alcohol. Allow the mixture to steep for four to six weeks, shaking it every few days. Add more alcohol if it's needed to keep the plant material covered.

To use, add the liquid to a spray bottle and lightly mist your hair and body. You can leave any remaining liquid and plant material inside the jar to continue steeping so the scent can deepen, but be sure to keep the plant material covered at all times with alcohol to prevent spoiling.

Playful Jasmine Tincture Perfume

The one thing we have in abundance in Los Angeles is citrus trees: it seems as though nearly every home, apartment, and sometimes business has a lemon, orange or grapefruit tree that produces fruit nearly all year long. Come spring these trees are bursting with the most fragrant blossoms that make a truly bright, floral and sensual perfume.

If you have any kind of citrus tree then gathering the blossoms will truly be worth the effort, but if not this recipe is lovely with just lemon and orange peel. One thing you really can't skip out on are fresh jasmine flowers: dried jasmine just doesn't compete in terms of fragrance. If fresh jasmine flowers aren't available (check with your local florist or garden center), then omit the flowers and instead add 20 drops of jasmine absolute to the final product.

- ½ cup lemon peel, preferably organic, chopped
- ½ cup orange peel, preferably organic, chopped
- ½–1 cup fresh jasmine flowers
- ½ cup orange or lemon blossoms, optional
- vodka or perfumer's alcohol

Be sure to wash the lemons and oranges well before chopping the peel to remove any dust or dirt. When peeling, try to avoid the white pithy part underneath. Allow the peels to dry overnight to reduce their water content. The flowers should also be gently washed and allowed to dry overnight.

Add the citrus peels, jasmine flowers and citrus blossoms if using to a jar and completely cover with vodka or perfumer's alcohol. Allow the mixture to steep for four to six weeks, shaking it every few days. Add more alcohol if needed to keep the plant material covered.

To use, add the liquid to a spray bottle and lightly mist your hair and body. You can leave any remaining liquid and plant material inside the jar to continue steeping so the scent can deepen, but be sure to keep the plant material covered at all times with alcohol to prevent spoiling.

Power perfume

I took the beauty archetype quiz myself and received the sovereign as one of my top two archetypes. I never really thought of myself as a sovereign energy until a few years ago, right around the time I made this perfume. In fact, this perfume was born out of a time when I really wanted to feel more worthy and confident in myself, so when I got the sovereign my mind immediately went to this recipe and I knew it needed to be in this book. It's a deep, sensual and slightly herbaceous fragrance of soft florals and warm vetiver. Normally I use vodka for spray scents, but I've used gin here as it has a much richer fragrance.

- 18 drops of vetiver essential oil
- 36 drops of jasmine absolute
- 9 drops of clary sage essential oil
- 3 oz | 90 ml jasmine floral water
- 1 oz | 30 ml gin

Combine all of the ingredients in a spray bottle. To use, shake gently to redistribute the oils and mist all over your body and hair.

THE WILD ONE EARTHY PERFUME

This recipe may seem weird and totally unexpected, but if you're into earthy, herbaceous, wild scents – I'm looking at you, wild one archetype – then you won't want to skip out on this one. Tarragon has a sharp, almost licorice-like scent that's grounded further by black tea. Neroli rounds out this blend with a pop of bright, fresh and floral scent. If nothing else you'll have a truly unique fragrance.

- 1 bunch of fresh tarragon
- 2 tbs black tea
- vodka or perfumer's alcohol
- $^1/_4$–$^1/_2$ tsp neroli essential oil

Allow the tarragon to dry overnight to reduce its water content, then roughly chop. Add the chopped tarragon and black tea to a jar and completely cover with the vodka or perfumer's alcohol. Allow the mixture to steep for four to six weeks, shaking it every few days. Add more alcohol if needed to keep the plant material covered.

To use, add 4 oz | 120 ml liquid and some of the neroli essential oil, adjusting to your desired scent level, to a spray bottle and lightly mist your hair and body. You can leave any remaining liquid and plant material inside the jar to continue steeping so the scent can deepen, but be sure to keep the plant material covered at all times with alcohol to prevent spoiling.

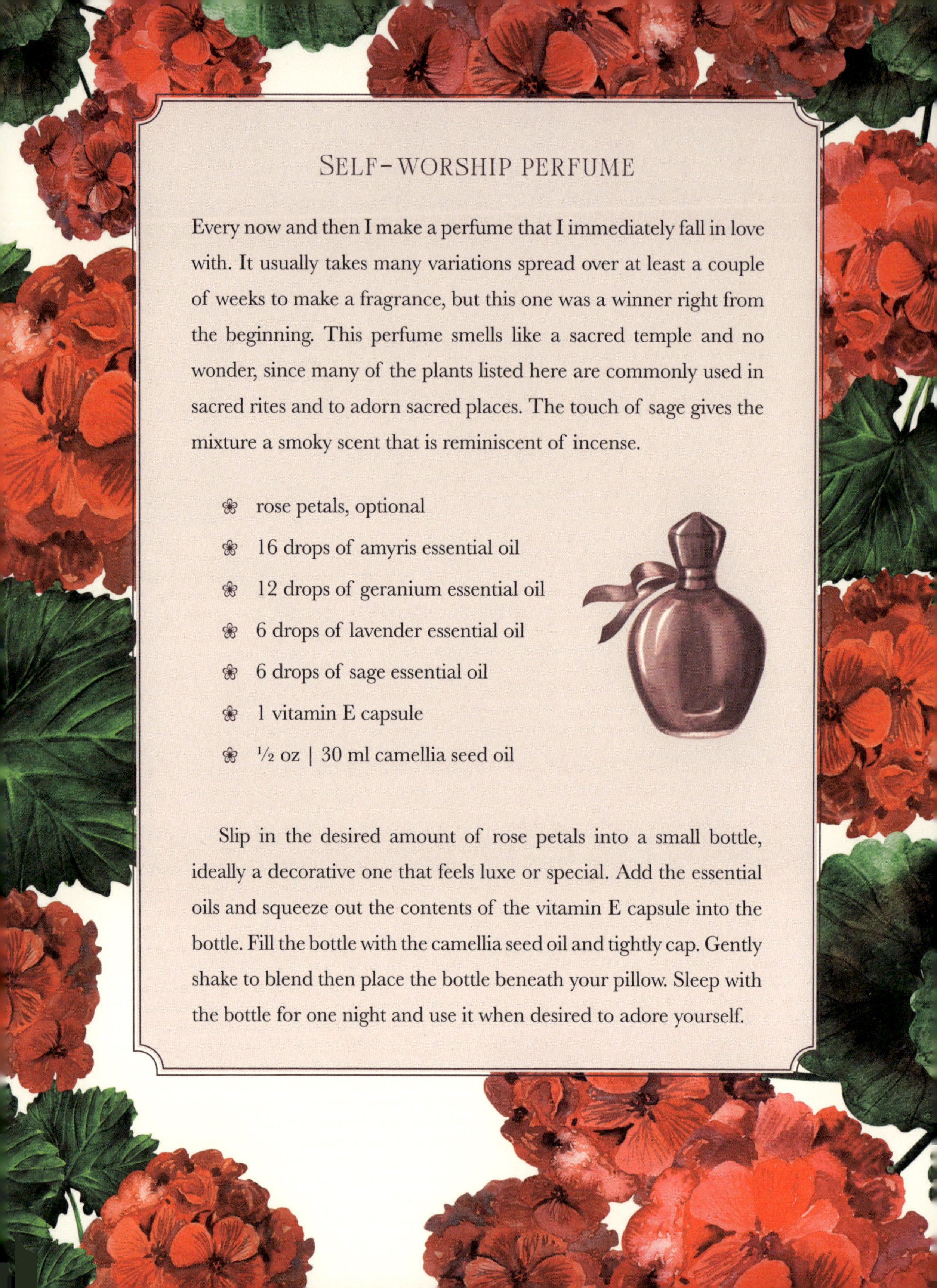

Self-worship perfume

Every now and then I make a perfume that I immediately fall in love with. It usually takes many variations spread over at least a couple of weeks to make a fragrance, but this one was a winner right from the beginning. This perfume smells like a sacred temple and no wonder, since many of the plants listed here are commonly used in sacred rites and to adorn sacred places. The touch of sage gives the mixture a smoky scent that is reminiscent of incense.

- rose petals, optional
- 16 drops of amyris essential oil
- 12 drops of geranium essential oil
- 6 drops of lavender essential oil
- 6 drops of sage essential oil
- 1 vitamin E capsule
- ½ oz | 30 ml camellia seed oil

Slip in the desired amount of rose petals into a small bottle, ideally a decorative one that feels luxe or special. Add the essential oils and squeeze out the contents of the vitamin E capsule into the bottle. Fill the bottle with the camellia seed oil and tightly cap. Gently shake to blend then place the bottle beneath your pillow. Sleep with the bottle for one night and use it when desired to adore yourself.

Honey Vanilla Perfume

I will never get over vanilla-infused oil, and I'm always on the hunt to find new ways to turn it into a perfume. Vanilla is a common ingredient in perfume because it brings a unifying and grounding scent to a blend. It works well with just about anything and it's said that wearing a dab of vanilla makes you seem more beautiful, so I absolutely had to include another vanilla bean perfume. This perfume is so warm and vibrant. You can make this recipe with vanilla extract, and you can replace the infused jojoba oil with vodka to which has been added ½ tsp of vanilla extract.

FOR THE VANILLA BEAN-INFUSED OIL:

- 3–4 vanilla bean pods, split lengthwise
- 1 cup jojoba oil

FOR THE PERFUME:

- 18 drops of bergamot essential oil
- 12 drops of petitgrain essential oil
- 9 drops of sweet orange essential oil
- 4 drops of honey

Add the vanilla bean pods and jojoba oil to a small crockpot or double broiler, chopping the beans if necessary to ensure they're completely covered. Cook on low for two to three hours, then remove from the heat and allow to cool. Strain the mixture and store it in a dark bottle or container with a tight-fitting lid.

To make the perfume, mix the essential oils with the honey in a small bowl until well combined, then mix in ½ oz | 15 ml of the vanilla bean–infused jojoba oil. Pour or spoon the mixture into a small bottle or container and tightly cap. To use, dab a small amount onto your pulse points and inhale deeply. Reapply throughout the day as needed.

The Empress perfume

I used to make this perfume through my brand Spirit Element, but one of the oils I used became unavailable. It was a special ingredient because it was completely natural, and one that was meant to replicate the fragrance of gardenia using extracts and other essential oils. It's taken me a long time to be able to replicate the perfume without the unavailable ingredient, and while it isn't perfect it's about 99 percent there. This perfume was inspired by The Empress tarot card, which represents all things beauty, abundance, and nurturing.

- 7 drops of patchouli essential oil
- 7 drops of ylang ylang essential oil
- 6 drops of neroli essential oil
- 4 drops of cardamom essential oil
- 3 drops of geranium essential oil
- 1 drop of jasmine essential oil
- 1 drop of rose essential oil
- ½ oz | 15 ml rosehip oil

Mix the essential oils with the rosehip oil in a small bowl until combined. Pour or spoon the mixture into a small bottle or container and tightly cap it.

To use, dab a small amount onto your pulse points and inhale deeply. Reapply throughout the day as needed.

Floral Creme and Spice Botanical Perfume

Infusing essential oils is one of my absolute favorite things to do, because it adds an unexpected scent profile that isn't quite the same as mixing essential oils together. Infusing an essential oil is very similar to making a tincture, although it doesn't last as long. Some essential oils are better at preserving than others; for example, I have a bottle of vanilla-infused cedarwood oil that I have had for more than a year and it still smells great.

- 1 vanilla bean
- ¼ tsp pink peppercorn
- 2 oz | 30 ml geranium essential oil
- 10 drops of rose essential oil
- 5 drops of jasmine essential oil
- 1 drop of cedarwood
- 1 oz | 30 ml jojoba oil

Split the vanilla bean in half lengthwise, then cut it in half horizontally. Put the pieces in a small bottle along with the pink peppercorn. Pour the geranium essential oil into the bottle, cap it and shake well. Allow the aromas to combine for two weeks.

Mix together 20 drops of the infused geranium oil, the remaining essential oils, and the jojoba oil in a small bowl. Pour or spoon the mixture into a small bottle or container and tightly cap it. To use, dab a small amount onto your pulse points and inhale deeply. Reapply throughout the day as needed.

CREATING BEAUTIFUL SPACE

Begin by focusing on bringing in four of the five senses – sight, scent, touch, and sound – into your space. Each one offers a plethora of intentional portals that can make your space feel much more aligned with the energy of beauty.

Sight

Your décor is the most obvious way to establish beauty in your space. Rather than focusing on trends or trying to force your style into one category, fill your space with things you love and that bring you joy: memorabilia, colors, patterns, shapes, artwork, and other decorative pieces all represent an opportunity to align with your version of beauty. If you need some inspiration refer back to your beautiful mind journal prompts on page 77, especially the ones in the everyday beauty category (page 80).

If your version of beauty is more aligned with the earth then you might choose organic shapes and natural fabrics and decorate your space with dried flowers and various curios, or perhaps you might even try making some of the furniture or décor yourself using items found in nature.

I recently stumbled across the Instagram page (@livefreelaurad) of a woman whose home didn't have walls. She lives completely immersed in nature and even has plants growing in her kitchen. When it comes to bugs, she has learned to live with them. In fact, she described the tiny bees that were leaving little piles of honey in all her drawers. This lifestyle isn't for everyone, but it absolutely represents the idea of a harmonious and beautiful life: Laura is in total alignment with who she is and the goals she's calling into existence.

The practice: think about what your highest, most beautiful self would want in your home. If your idea of beauty is having a very clean, minimalist home, start inviting some of that into your space now. If you eventually want to live in the countryside, start incorporating elements you might have in your future farmhouse.

You may not be in the space or even city you want just yet, but you can start to draw that energy in by using your space to hold your vision. If, for example, you want to live without walls in your home you can start by hanging artwork of the woods or beach or whatever landscape you imagine that future existing in. When you look at this art stop for a moment and imagine there are no walls, and with time you will train yourself to naturally gravitate toward things that feel beautiful for you.

Touch

Textures are such an easy and tactile way to bring beauty into your space. In fact, fabric is how this concept started for me. A few years ago I began taking steps to only put natural fabrics on my skin. I thought about what my future self would want, and she wanted to be mindful of what types of material she subjected her skin to. It was an act of self-care in the sense that I didn't want to wear scratchy or irritating fabrics, and I also wanted to invest in my style by purchasing quality pieces that could stand up to the test of time. I started replacing synthetic fabrics with organic ones such as cotton, linen, and silk, including my sheets, pillows, and the fabrics of my furniture.

It didn't take long for me to decide I wanted to have natural materials in my entire house. When I look for pieces of furniture I'll touch regularly now I intentionally choose woods, rattan, cork, and other organic materials. To me these things represent luxury and beauty, because I believe wealthy people can be more selective about what they purchase. If I were wealthy I would only have natural materials. I may not be able to redo my house from top to bottom and I certainly still have inorganic clothes and materials in my home, but I'm slowly taking steps to shift toward having more things that represent beauty and accomplishment for me.

The practice: every time I sit on wood furniture or sleep on linen sheets I get a little excited, knowing I'm one step closer to being the person I want to be and expressing my identity in the way I wish to express it. You can do the same: if fabrics such as fur, linen, and suede represent beauty for you, start by adding lower-ticket items like throw pillows, curtains, or even very small items such as a diary. If you want more beauty and passion between you and your partner you might think about changing out sheets that are silky or tossing blankets on the couch for snuggling. You can even give attention to flooring and the texture of the walls, door knobs, drawer pulls, and fixtures.

Scent

I am a firm believer that a home should have a signature scent, just like you might have a signature perfume. People always say my home smells so good when they come over, and that's because I have diffusers running every single day. Over the years I have found myself making a signature scent for every season.

You may not have a signature scent yet but perhaps you might find one in this book, and you can absolutely infuse your home with various fragrances of your choice. Essential oils have spiritual properties that can be mixed to infuse your space with the energy you're wishing to call in.

While fragrance oils do not have energetic properties, they still contribute to your sense of well-being and add a beautiful scent. Just like textures and décor, certain scents – natural or not – invoke a feeling. Florals might represent love for you, or woods might represent well-being and stability. Fresh scents may represent cleanliness or happiness, and perhaps spices represent coziness. It doesn't really matter what someone else says a fragrance represents: if it invokes a desired feeling in you then use it.

The practice: go to your favorite home décor store and smell various candle scents. Close your eyes and inhale the scent deeply. What does the scent make you think of? Do you feel comforted and peaceful? Do you feel energized? Was there a scent you imagine a beautiful person would have in their home? Was there a scent you imagined a home in St Tropez would smell like?

Fill your home with the scent of the candle that smells most in alignment with your goals. Don't just stop at candles: also try sprays, air fresheners, and simmer pots, and even consider the scent of the foods you prepare.

Sound

Noise makes a world of difference to how you live. If you are seeking more beauty and peace, then loud, busy music may not help you accomplish this goal. Consider the background noise of your home: you might play records, turn on nature sounds, or listen to your favorite shows while you go about your day.

The practice: turn off everything in your home, every electronic device and anything that makes noise. Open the windows and listen to the noise outside. Do you hear a lot of traffic or people in the neighborhood? Are there birds chirping and dogs barking? Do these sounds represent the way you wish to live? If so then great, but if not you may need to start thinking about ways to drown out the sound.

If possible, choose high-quality windows that help reduce noise. Of course, that isn't accessible to many, including myself, but here are some other ways to cut down on noise from outdoors:

- Purchase soundproof window inserts.
- Hang curtains with heavy fabrics.
- Seal any holes or gaps in the walls, windows, and floorboards.
- Place bookshelves and large furniture against outer walls. Books especially help to buffer noise.
- Use area rugs and runners on hardwood and tile floors or install carpet.
- Plant shrubs and trees along the perimeter of your property.
- Use weather stripping along windows and doors.

Once you have buffered the outside sound you can deliberately choose music or melody that appeals to your sense of beautiful sound. YouTube has so many options for every kind of sound you can imagine: spiritual clearing videos, religious chants, peaceful homes, videos to make your house sound like Hogwarts or a classical music hall on Santorini. Search it and you will find it, but you can also find nature sounds on platforms such as Spotify or purchase and play records.

BEAUTIFUL HOME FRAGRANCES

To make the following blends, add the essential oils to a bottle, cap it and shake well. Allow the mixture to synergize for one to two days. Add 5 to 15 drops of the blend to your aromatherapy diffuser to infuse your space with the beautiful fragrance and healing energy. You can also add the essential oils straight to a diffuser but the scent will be slightly different and a little less harmonious, although still enjoyable.

Self-awareness diffuser blend

- 8 drops of cypress essential oil
- 8 drops of fennel essential oil
- 5 drops of rosemary essential oil

Self-identity diffuser blend

- 16 drops of rose essential oil
- 2 drops of cypress essential oil
- 8 drops of cananga essential oil

Self-confidence diffuser blend

- 5 drops of basil essential oil
- 8 drops of bergamot essential oil
- 4 drops of cedar essential oil
- 4 drops of geranium essential oil

Self-compassion diffuser blend

- 10 drops of neroli essential oil
- 10 drops of sweet marjoram essential oil

Self-worth diffuser blend

- 5 drops of neroli essential oil
- 2 drops of jasmine fragrance
- 5 drops of bergamot essential oil

Self-trust diffuser blend

- 12 drops of lavender essential oil
- 2 drops of lemongrass essential oil
- 7 drops of hemlock spruce essential oil

Self-serenity diffuser blend

- 4 drops of angelica essential oil
- 7 drops of amyris essential oil
- 15 drops of lavender essential oil
- 9 drops of spruce essential oil
- 15 drops of bergamot essential oil

Self-expression diffuser blend

- 10 drops of geranium essential oil
- 6 drops of neroli essential oil
- 2 drops of jasmine absolute oil
- 1 drop of palma rosa essential oil

Self-devotion diffuser blend

- 86 drops of amyris essential oil
- 24 drops of geranium essential oil
- 6 drops of rose essential oil

BIBLIOGRAPHY

Blankenship, Jana, 2019, *Wild Beauty: Wisdom & recipes for natural self-care*, Ten Speed Press, New York, USA

Buck, Shannon, 2014, *200 Tips, Techniques & Recipes for Natural Beauty*, Fair Winds Press, Massachusetts, USA

Dugliss-Wesselman, Stacey, 2013, *The Home Apothecary*, Quarry Books, New York, USA

Groves, Maria Noël, 2016, *Body into Balance: An herbal guide to holistic self-care*, Storey Publishing, Massachusetts, USA

Kynes, Sandra, 2019, *Llewellyn's Complete Book of Essential Oils: How to blend, diffuse, create remedies, and use in everyday life*, Llewellyn Publications, Minnesota, USA

Kynes, Sandra, 2013, *Mixing Essential Oils for Magic: Aromatic alchemy for personal blends*, Llewellyn Publications, Minnesota, USA

Kynes, Sandra, 2013, *Llewellyn's Complete Book of Correspondences: a comprehensive & cross referenced resource for pagans & wiccans*, Llewellyn Publications, Minnesota, USA

Kynes, Sandra, 2017, *Plant Magic: a year of green wisdom for pagans & wiccans*, Llewellyn Publications, Minnesota, USA

McCoy, Anya, 2018, *Homemade Perfume: Create exquisite, naturally scented products to fill your life with botanical aromas*, Page Street Publishing, Massachusetts, USA

Panton, Sara, 2019, *Essential Well Being: a modern guide to using essential oils in beauty, body and home rituals*, Penguin Random House, Canada

Vadhera, Shalini, 2006, *Passport to Beauty: Secrets and tips from around the world for becoming a global goddess*, St Martin's Griffin, New York, USA

Worwood, Valerie Anne, 1991, *The Complete Book of Essential Oils & Aromatherapy*, New World Library, California, USA

ABOUT THE AUTHOR

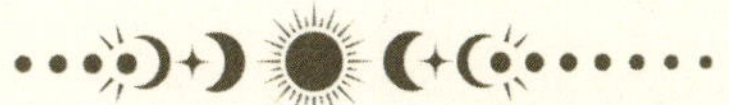

Lorriane Anderson is a multidisciplinary spiritual teacher, writer, and soul-based entrepreneur whose work focuses heavily on intentional and energetic living as well as using spiritual practices as a pathway for profound healing, growth, and transformation. She has been featured in *The Daily Star*, *The Spruce*, *Reader's Digest*, *Kindred Spirit*, *Oprah Daily*, and *VoyageLA* among others. She is the author of *The Witch's Apothecary* and *The Moon Apothecary*, as well as several other titles in the spiritual space, and is co-creator of the bestselling *Seasons of the Witch* oracle deck series.

SPIRITELEMENT.CO | @SPIRITELEMENT

ALSO IN THIS SERIES

The Witch's Apothecary

ISBN: 9781925946796

The Moon Apothecary

ISBN: 9781925946802

AVAILABLE NOW FROM ALL GOOD BOOKSTORES

ROCKPOOLPUBLISHING.COM